BERKSHIRE
BYWAYS

BERKSHIRE
BYWAYS

PETER DAVIES

THE HISTORY PRESS

First published in the United Kingdom in 2008 by
The History Press
Cirencester Road · Chalford · Stroud · Gloucestershire · GL6 8PE

British Library Cataloguing in Publication Data
A catalogue record for this book is available from the British Library.

ISBN 978-0-7509-4960-6

To Jim

*Who has rescued me from the jaws of my computer
many times.*

Typeset in 11/13.5pt Sabon.
Typesetting and origination by
The History Press.
Printed and bound in England.

Contents

	Introduction	7
1	Going Downhill on a Bicycle	9
2	A Cursory View of the Area	13
3	Onward & Ockward	18
4	Aldermaston March	27
5	A Walk to Yattendon in Snow	37
6	Civil War & Civil Disobedience	41
7	Hamstead Marshall	64
8	The Museum	70
9	Muscle Up!	73
10	From One Green Valley to Another	78
11	Looping the Loop	90
12	Ariel & Skylarks: Riding on Air	92
	Epilogue: Nature's Spring Flower Show	122
	A Berkshire Bibliography	124
	Acknowledgements	128

The River Kennet where it enters Berkshire at Chilton Foliat.

A gypsy camp on the Ridgeway.

Introduction

Not lost, simply diverted

If I were to list my principal hobbies, I would include gawping: not idly or uselessly, but with awe. And Berkshire offers plenty to be awestruck about. First there is the ancient trackway of the Ridgeway. Is there a more splendid walk in the world? Alternatively one can cycle easily the whole length of the Kennet and Avon Canal. In between, beyond and below, are a hundred grand spectacles, natural and manmade. This book takes in as many as nature and the man who made it would allow. But, beside all that, there are the wonderful spontaneous delights and discoveries that await the open-minded – and the open-mouthed – traveller, as well as the chance encounters with people. Thus we have the splendour of Abingdon's sixteenth-century Town Hall and the man on the Ock river path confidently expecting another Ice Age; the discovery that Newbury was the first town in England to have Belisha beacons, that an Aldermaston schoolmaster produced the famous William pear, that another William, surnamed Plenty, invented an early lifeboat, or that in 1607 William Rush 'ballooned' down from the tower of Lambourn church in a four-masted pinnace – a kind of flying boat – on a fantastic journey which took him via the Thames all the way to London.

The Ridgeway and the waterways are at the heart of the book, providing perhaps the key to the richness of this superlative county with its ancient – and modern – royal connections, its ancient downland much favoured by racehorses, their owners and trainers; by sheep, shepherds and farmers; by golfers, balloonists and strollers alike.

And much of it is free!

Going Downhill on a Bicycle

With lifted feet, hands still,
I am poised, and down the hill
Dart, with heedful mind;
The air goes by in a wind.

Swifter, and yet more swift,
Till the heart with a mighty lift
Makes the lungs laugh, the throat cry:
'O bird see; see, bird, I fly;

Is this, is this your joy?
O bird, then I, though a boy,
For a golden moment share
Your feathery life in air.'

Say, heart, is there aught like this
In a world that is full of bliss?
'Tis more than skating, bound
steel-shod to the level ground.

Speed slackens now, I float
Awhile in my airy boat;
Till, when the wheels scarce crawl,
My feet to the treadles fall.

Alas, that the longest hill
Must end in a vale; but still
Who climbs with toil, wheresoe'er,
Shall find wings waiting there.

H.C. Beeching

CHAPTER ONE

Going Downhill on a Bicycle

What a title! And what a treat have we in store! No one since R.L. Stevenson had so well caught the sense of excitement that grips the heart of a boy when he first senses the freedom of 'going like the wind'. Edwardian children's authors like J.M. Barrie and A.A. Milne seemed to write for boys permanently arrested in their development, aged six; but here was one who effortlessly conveyed exultation in the breasts of boys of all ages. Apart from a ''tis' here and a 'whatsoe'er' there, he matched very naturally the experience with the words used to describe it. 'Treadles' is no real obstacle, since many machines were foot-operated in those days – the early twentieth century; but it does, for the first time perhaps strike a slightly odd note, setting the author at a less comfortable distance from the reader. Perish the thought that that bike was a fixed-wheel, borrowed perhaps by a Yattendon boy from his grandfather in Frilsham, and that he may have been giving one of his friends a ride on the bar!

The author's garden at Frilsham.

The way through the woods.

It is most unlikely that the boy was the author, the Revd H.C. Beeching, Rector of Yattendon and subsequently Canon of Norwich Cathedral. He is remembered in the Revd J.E. Smith-Master's book on Yattendon as 'one of the Church of England's noblest sons,' and, as a poet, fit to stand beside John Donne, George Herbert or Andrew Marvell. *The Oxford Book of English Verse* doesn't quote him – but then it has scant room for those other poets associated with Yattendon, and Beeching's near-contemporaries, Henry Newbolt and Robert Bridges.

Certainly I often think of him when I hurtle down Coombe Hill on my bike of many gears – my speed only a fraction of Beckham's swerve or Henman's serve – with my dog deliberately lagging behind, unimpressed. I can confirm that Beeching's open-air tonic for boys of all ages really works. I arrive at the shop in Yattendon and the lady says, 'Good morning, young man!'

Returning, however, the converse is true. Stumbling up Coombe Hill I am more likely to be behind my dog and muttering, 'Say not the struggle nought availeth,' or old Henry Newbolt's *Vitai Lampada* (that, too, sounds like medicine): 'Play up, play up and play the game!'

Green Moonbeams.

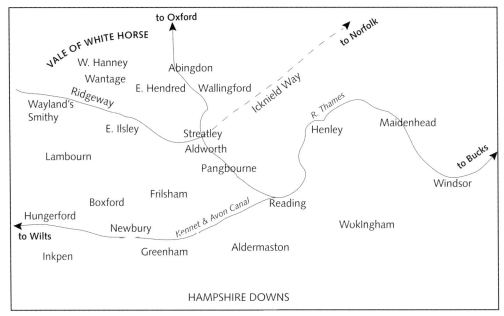

My map of Berkshire is shaped like a long envelope, stamped, I am pleased to say, with more then one royal seal.

Along the northern edge runs the Vale of White Horse and the Ridgeway which does not end at Streatley but goes on as the Icknield Way to run out at Hunstanton on the Norfolk coast.

The Thames marks, erratically, the eastern edge, running on to Windsor, London and out to sea.

To the south are the Kennet & Avon Canal and the transverse ridges – you can hardly called them hills – that mount up to the Hampshire Downs.

The western edge extends to the chalk downlands of Wiltshire. The whole envelope, noted for its whiteness, is the remains of an ancient inland sea.

CHAPTER TWO

A Cursory View of the Area

I have just been given a 1:1000 map of Frilsham. I had no idea what an eye-opener it would be. It is like seeing one's own fingerprints under a powerful magnifying glass. What is personal suddenly appears outlandishly strange. What was thought to be familiar seems almost surreal. For instance, in this map is revealed the identities of all our miscellaneous woods. What poetry is in their names! I knew we had High Copse, Coombe Wood and Hawkridge Wood; but now I see we have, alongside them, Sulham's Copse, Franklin's Copse, Nightingale's Copse, Cook's Copse, Plee Copse, Whitmore Copse and – down below them – Quavies and Little Quavies, eventually petering out into No Man's Land. Oaken Copse, north of Yattendon, and the Alders, above Hawkridge are self-explanatory; but who would not wish to investigate Little Gray's Copse and nearby Wynalls (unpossessed) Copse; or, over there in the west, Little Cholseys Copse (again without an apostrophe), Long Groys, Geoff's Corner, Spring Plantation, Pimbus Shaw and – most intriguing of all – Damaskfield Copse? Think of the birdsong! Think of the spring flowers: wood sorrel, spurge, archangel, windflowers, violets, primroses and, of course, bluebells – all embowered by beeches breaking into leaf! Alone, the brimstone emulates the frail luminosity of soft, yellow-green beech leaves. They last about as long; but, for a brief spell of transfiguration, they represent Berkshire at its breath-taking best.

Wherever you go in Frilsham you go down hill – then climb back up again. You nose-dive out, like the rooks from the trees. It is most exhilarating on a bike. Westwards you drop down to Stanford Dingley or Lower Bucklebury; eastwards, to Hawkridge and Lower Frilsham – all resting in the arm of the River Pang.

Berkshire is all rivers and fertile chalkland left by an ancient Pliocene sea. It is from the rivers that Berkshire's rural and industrial prosperity and resources mainly spring. The Ock, the first to flow into the Thames at Abingdon, takes us to the north of the county; but to fully investigate it we need to look west at Farringdon, once a premier market town – and nearby Great Coxwell where the tithe barn tells its own story of royal endowment and ecclesiastical munificence.

The beautiful River Dun.

A typical bridge on the Kennet & Avon Canal.

The Vale of White Horse, King Alfred's home turf and the centre of racing country, occupy a large part of that old Pliocene sea-bed, scooped out by glaciers many thousands of years ago. The arc of the Ridgeway helps to define our northern course.

To the south are the Pang, the Lambourn, the Dun and the Kennet with its attendant canal to the Thames at Reading. The Kennet and Avon Canal was

Curious bison at Hermitage.

once a trade route that ran like a blue ribbon between Bristol in the west to Gravesend in the east but now, along with that other important trade route of the more distant past, the Ridgeway, has become a freeway for leisured people like me. Ultimately, it is the waterways and ancient green roads that have given Berkshire its precedence among English inland counties, making it what it is: royal, ancient and free.

These are my thoughts as I sit at home in Frilsham, scanning my maps, plotting my course, watching the weather – and changing my mind. Shh! We do not really know where Berkshire's limits lie, or which route we'll take next, so long as it unfrequented, fair and free.

Three brotherly bulls in a neighbouring field.

CHAPTER THREE

Onward & Ockward

My map tells me that the River Ock runs eastward from Great Coxwell, whose massive tithe barn is one of the prizes of this trip. This little-known and, therefore most interesting river eventually joins the Thames at Abingdon, which is another attraction to me. Before the boundary changes of 1974, the Vale of White Horse with its transverse hills and rivers formed a natural divide between Berkshire and Oxfordshire to which many of the people who live there still adhere; and, since history and geography chiefly interest me, I will go along with that. We, who run free, are not ruled by postcodes. In any case, if we regard the Ridgeway as the rim of the pot – this bowl of plenty which we call Berkshire – we may equally well regard the Vale of White Horse as the lid, however hard a struggle we may have to keep it on!

The struggle for me begins in the New Year. High winds and rain from the Atlantic nearly scupper my plans, but, full of resolution, I am determined to proceed. New Year's Eve sees Hogmanay washed out in Edinburgh and many of England's more feeble revels abandoned. Huddled indoors on Monday 1 January, I cravenly plot an assault on the Pang. Tuesday is fine. I have only to cycle to Bradfield, then walk the course to where it joins the Thames at Pangbourne. Easier said than done. . .

Bradfield is only a stone's throw from home and mostly downhill. It is famous, like so many key places on my itinerary – Pangbourne, Abingdon, Reading, Wantage and, of course, Eton for its school. The church is tucked away beyond the mill and its accompanying 'conversions' which all look incidental today. Where, you wonder, do the villagers live? The answer seems to be an offshoot or siding at Southend beyond the powerhouse of learning which monopolises the hill. I meet no one who can tell me where the public footpath leads from the village down to the river flowing east, although the one to the west is well-marked and much frequented by people and their dogs. I cross over the road, facing the sun at this early hour, and blunder into what looks like a cut which, of course, peters out. I can see the river racing ahead but a huge sports centre and car park stands between me and the top road which, I guess runs parallel to the river for a time. There, somehow, I find a gateway into a field, leave the bike locked in a thicket of brambles, and head airily down to the stream. There is no one about. My old poaching insincts tell me that there will be a well-mown fisherman's path running right alongside the free-flowing Pang, even in the close season – and there is. It leads to a dead-end, an island of scrub willow and a track across a plough field to a distant farm. I keep to the headland which follows the river almost to the motorway. Another farm, screened by a cypress hedge and visited by a post van, indicates that there must be a way out. A footbridge, no less, takes me over the crazy behemoth, to a footpath wondrously marked – the first I have seen – which leads by ever more wondrous markings (by DEFRA) to Tidmarsh. Here, Macadam rules. Tidmarsh Grange is under development: Camelot, it seems from the architect's blown-up roadside designs. 'Sixteen mansions and five acres of woodland.' Only a blank, distempered tower with pretentious crenellations, takes it out of Disneyland into the realm of King Arthur, making me laugh. Welcome, then, to the Greyhound on the corner and the mill, opposite which is a real-life pony and trap heading for the bridge and the path which will assuredly lead me across the fields to Sulham and, eventually, to Pangbourne. It is photograph time. The driver of the pony obliges. The river,

The Greyhound, Tidmarsh.

Bramble Cottage, Sulham.

lazily coursing across meadows, obliges. Bramble Cottage obliges. Nothing
can go wrong now. I fetch up at the Star in Pangbourne and drink a pint of
ale. It is half past twelve. All I have to do is see where the Pang pours into the
Thames, turn round and go home. Easier said than done. . .

Retracing my steps, I study more carefully the mill at Tidmarsh where
Lytton Strachey famously lived: 'grinding,' I mumble to myself, 'no more than
a preposition, I doubt.' Polyanthus are in full flower by the locked iron gates. I
pluck an ash plant from the roadside further on and head for the fields again.
That designated path is truly marvellous, though now uphill. I am heading
west, into the sun and into the wind – always exhilarating. Tidmarsh Manor
stands white-gabled and sun-splashed high on a ridge. Another magnificent
house with tall chimneys – a sign of wealth in the old days – stands, screened
by a belt of beech trees, away from the motorway. Over the footbridge –
presumably by permission – over a farm gate and on past the cypresses and
over the fields I go to join the brimming river again. Shots ring out. I strike
across the plough land, tacky with mud. More shots volley and thunder. I am
heading right into the firing zone. The river has here been expanded into
fishing lakes. A man is standing on the far side of one, his back to me. I try to

The River Pang.

make myself invisible. What if he turns? No, he is shooting into the wood beyond. Pheasants? I quickly regain the fisherman's path. There, facing me, is Indiana Jones, his gun under one arm and a plump hen pheasant, its neck freshly wrung, on the end of the other.

'I'm trying to find the correct path back to Bradfield,' I pant.

'Oh, the paths go everywhere and anywhere, here,' he smiles, happy no doubt with his bird. Under his waterproof cladding and his broad-brimmed, leathery hat, he displays a kind of human vulnerability. Much relieved, I trespass on, soon reach the road and rejoin my bike. 'My dainty Ariel,' I cry, releasing him from the indignity of being padlocked to a briar, and pedal home.

The Ock, At Last

In the beginning was the Ock, but time and the weather has altered its course. And mine. But we are not thinking of days. We have suddenly to adjust to geological time. Some thousands, if not millions of years. Back to the last ice age, in fact. If you believe what the books say, the most extensive glaciations covered Britain as far as the Thames Valley and the Bristol Channel, so that when the ice melted parts of Southern England became a sort of isthmus between the Atlantic and the North Sea.

After the ice retreated the land rose slowly in relation to the sea level resulting in the 'upwarping' of hills, the gradual formation of a network of rivers – some changing course completely, like the Severn, and the unimaginable crash of the Thames downhill through the Goring Gap. Bemused by all this, it is quite comforting to take to the manageable, fordable Ock – the first in my simple scheme of Thames tributaries to get the process under way.

My revised plan is to join it at Lyford and walk along it to Garford, Frilford and Abingdon; but in the second week of January the westerlies are still raging and flood warnings are out on Macadamised roads. The wellingtons stay in the car. Plan B says concentrate on churches, a favourite pastime of mine. Denchworth has been recommended. There is an inn – and, across the road from the inn, a surprise. Nay, more than a surprise, a complete step back in time. The little stone church, stubby-towered, sits in a green acre of its own, totally secluded, lost to the world. The key is brought for me by a lady in the village. She recommends that I give the old door a good shove. She does not hurry away but beams with obvious pride at what we see inside, all so beautifully kept. A 1541 Bible of Cranmer's is displayed under glass and out of the light. I trace with my twentieth-century index finger the sixteenth-century print. The Prophesye of Nahum – have I heard of him? Ah yes,

Denchworth Church.

'Beholde upon the mountain come the feet of him that bringeth good tidynges and preacheth peace.'

I go on to Charney Manor – occupied, the sign says, by the Religious Society of Friends. Aconites, like a string of little gold lights, line the base of the warm Cotswoldy wall. There is a church of similarly smiling stone; but I have been spoilt by Denchworth – and the sun-loving aconites have reinfected me with a taste for the out-of-doors. I travel on, deceiving myself that I am actually splashing footfirst through the sun-splashed, rain-splashed valley of the Ock. Before I know where I am, I am in Abingdon. I find easy parking on the outskirts of town and step eagerly onto the street. And what a street! The numbers of the houses run well into the hundreds. It reminds me of Whitehall or the Embankment. It is called Ock Street; and, indeed, there somewhere behind all those Georgian and perhaps earlier inns, mills and other old, working premises – ignoring the clamour of the new – is the river, twinned with another unknown, the Stert, running into the arms of the Thames by St Helen's church.

I ignore the turn to the MG Club at Shippon and the one to the school, having nearly collided with a tousled-haired pair of boys riding two-on-a-bike, and head for the Town Hall, a tidy walk, as we country dwellers say.

St Helen's church, Abingdon.

*Abingdon
Town Hall.*

Where would you find another building so imposing, so set-apart, yet so central and functional at the same time as this town hall? It has all the solid rusticity you would expect of seventeenth-century Abingdon combined with the airy grace of the Taj Mahal. It is John Bull's Palace.

'By order of Mr Mayor,' an old notice proclaims, 'If any Person shall lay any Filth, Dirt or Rubbish on or upon any Part of the Market House, or by any Means whatsoever Daub or Damage it shall be punished to the Severity of the Law. And if any Person shall inform the Bellman of the same shall receive six pence.' What an emphatic enforcement by Capital Letter of the Law!

I am locked out of the parish church – and the Church Centre; so there is no seeing the fabled painted ceiling or one of the widest aisles in Christendom. But I have a trip down the Ock Valley Walk, encountering an engaging fellow who assures me – 'though the television doesn't tell you this' – that boats cause just as much pollution as aircraft, and that global warming has happened before, and that another ice age is probably on the way. It is a relief to regain the street and see one enormous mill (alas not practising) and the great Stratton Building, built by the same Tompkins, a wealthy Baptist family, who bequeathed multiple almshouses and other benefits to the town. Ah, civic pride! Ah, municipal grandeur! Ah, what price progress? –or even cleanliness? – in a toothless modern society when the Bellman cannot buy for sixpence the Severity of the Law!

CHAPTER FOUR

Aldermaston March

It is Candlemas, the feast of the Purification of the Virgin Mary and the presentation of Christ in the Temple. It is crocus time; revival time; reflection and renewal time. What better place to be visiting then than Aldermaston, a village with perhaps the strangest history – and the subject of most unwanted attention in the more recent past. So it is also reclamation time.

My map says that I can go by almost continuous footpaths nearly all the way. (Better than marching from London, I tell myself!) Cold Ordnance Survey print indicates – too enticingly to be believable – that I can go straight through Bucklebury to Midgham, across the Kennet, by Brimpton Mill, by Manor Farm and Wasing Lower Farm, then join the road into the village of Aldermaston itself. Also marked, is the course of the old Roman road.

The Rowbarge, Midgham.

The object of all this premeditation is to maximise the daylight – short enough in early February – and the time I spend in the village which Henry VIII and Elizabeth I, Bertrand Russell and Canon Collins and many other luminaries visited for one reason or another. I particularly want to see the church of St Mary the Virgin where the famous fourteenth-century *York Mystery Play* has been presented for the past fifty years consecutively; and what better time of year to do so than at Candlemas?

I have books at home telling me about the play, which I have not yet seen but I believe without blasphemy may be as much a consolation for me as the actual presentation of the Baby Jesus was for Simeon in the Temple at Jerusalem.

Of almost as great interest to me is Aldermaston's superb village project for the millennium: a book entitled *Memories*. I am eager to meet Mrs Martin, the editor, and, if possible, some of the contributors.

In *Memories* you may read how the villagers viewed the savants of CND. 'The marchers used to camp on the green. They covered themselves with plastic to keep warm – it was Easter and quite cold. They were exhausted. . . . We had double-decker buses and coaches in the village – it was all very peaceful . . . the villagers used to give them cups of tea.' Another entry reads: 'The people walked so far their feet were bleeding. I remember seeing their feet covered in rags to stop the blood.'

And all because AEI (Associated Electrical Industries) developed the first nuclear reactor at the Court, visited by the Duke of Edinburgh in 1965, when, so one contributor says: 'All the girls working at the Court had to wear white shoes to look smart and not dusty! It was knocked down in later years and the new Blue Circle Cement offices were built on the site.'

Feet have figured large in Aldermaston's history. One thinks of the Roman soldiers marching by on their way to or from Silchester. One thinks of the many football teams raised in the village over the years; and the scores accumulated by the cricketers; and all the spadework that went into the annual produce show. And here is an entry which says: 'We used to have a "Show Marathon" . . . not a full marathon mind you, more of a fun run. . . . I had been serving in the Army in Malaya and when I returned I decided to enter. My brother Reg got onto me . . . said I'd never beat Ron Step, who was a well-known local runner. But he was wrong. Having just left the Army, I was very fit and have really been a runner all my life. Besides, Ron Step was in his fifties by then. . .'

And so to cricket, for which this village is justly and fundamentally famed, for it is the home of the Surridge cricket bat – that stout protector of many famous feet. 'We used to have the young fast bowlers down in the yard in the winter,' says David Luker, 'before they were picked for the England team . . .

Hawkridge Farm, Frilsham.

to toughen them up and get them fit. . . Frank Tyson, Alan Moss, Peter Loader. . . I would show them the whole cycle of growing, felling and sawing willow, ready for making into cricket bats. . .'

What down-to-earth stuff this is! It beats *Our Village* by Mary Russell Mitford and *Lark Rise to Candleford* by Flora Thompson and makes *Cider With Rosie* look like pale ale. I hope I arrive in the village with a good aggregate of Berkshire mud on my boots!

The River Pang, Bucklebury Ford.

Sunday 4 February, dawns, frosty-bright. The fields sparkle. The sky is criss-crossed by vapour trails which look less like the hellish omens of pollution than some sort of heavenly heraldry: chevrons and saltires, the argent tails of rampant Boeings that can sometimes be seen hurrying from or back to their dens at Heathrow. I nose-dive on my silver Elan through Hawkridge, down to the River Pang which has suddenly sprung to life. Sun dances on the water. I skip along with it, chuckling aqueously. There is nothing like a small river for company; it is like a small child, constantly cheerful and unaware of such artificial concepts as cold. Somewhere I lose my gloves – they just slide out of my pocket – but there is no going back – they are cheap, useless things, anyway. Travel light.

I am struck by some sort of white monsters stationed in a field, stretching onwards and upwards to the horizon. Plastic bales used to be black. 'Straw bales and vapour trails', I chant. The river and the sheep mumbling among turnips in the field opposite chant back. The sheep are ordinary Suffolks, as right-minded a breed as any; but this morning the sun bounces off their backs and gives them an almost skittish air. The Frilsham Chorale, I call them. Soon, I am at the ford, which for months was dry but is now full. Two chaps, out early, are testing the ice with their sticks, old men suddenly recovering their youth 'Perfect day!' Nothing more needs to be said.

Bucklebury church commands my attention. I wander in. People I meet in the graveyard tell me that the early service has just ended. They also tell me that this is a well-attended church. Even the cottages beside it look loved. My hand is clutched by the vicar, a personable fellow who has the sweetest smile and sincerest greeting I have encountered in ages. My eye lights on the gilded dedications on the gallery at the back to prominent benefactors in the past, among them John Winchcombe. 'Of the same family as Jack of Newbury,' I exclaim, with early-morning schoolboy brightness.

'Come to the ten o'clock service, and I'll give you a history lesson,' says a scholarly gent who is probably the church warden – 'got to go and get my breakfast now!' And I have to push on, or I would gladly wait till ten o'clock or later in this warm and welcoming place.

Soon, I have another church in view: that of Midgham. I have seen it many times from the south side where it looks down from the hill top onto the Bath road and the Kennet and Avon Canal. Now, for the first time I approach it from the back. But it is more commanding physically than it is spiritually. Its spire reaches way up into the blue. It is wholly imposing but piercing rather than striking ; it is cold and flinty; Victorian, I suppose. Somebody is making a statement without really telling you anything. Two men emerge from the main

Bucklebury church.

door and lock up. So my judgement cannot be reversed by the interior. I drop down to a car-crazy A4 and a quarry and land-fill site where I realise I have suffered a puncture. The tyre will not inflate. So what? It is still only ten o'clock. I cross the canal where two or three brave spirits are jogging on the tow-path or exercising their dogs. I decide to take the Brimpton road, see the mill, the chapel, the village – which lies curiously aloof and unintriguing. There is the busy little Kennet hurrying ceaselessly along, in contrast to some strange and straggling housing developments where, at this time on a Sunday, hardly anyone is up and about. Five cars to a bungalow, no garden to speak of, no apparent neighbourliness. I look up in despair, my front wheel bumping on the metalled road. 'Straw bales and vapour trails. . . .'

Wasing estate is extensive. Lower Farm retains some of its red Berkshire brick-and-tile glow. Some new development outside Aldermaston deflates the spirits – but only temporarily. The Hind's Head sees to that. Are there three centuries of architecture here? It is a puzzle. It is so enormous that you cannot take your eyes off it; you are in danger of being run over at the crossroads. This is no squalid village pub. This is an ancient hostelry, offering pilgrims hospitality; a place, like Bucklebury, to return to. Leave it then, the emblem of the hind dozing in the sun; climb the hill into the village; savour these walls (the peculiar feature of all estate villages); these loved cottages; the splendid Parish Hall ('licensed by Act of Parliament in the pursuance of Music, Singing and Dancing'); the altogether too-grand Court Gatehouse; the intricate and amusing instances of cross-brickwork on chimneys and gables; the long climb to the out-of- the- way church – walled and surrounded by yew, yielding glimpses only of the cedar-crowned park on one side and the valley of the Kennet on the other.

Leaving my disabled bike at the lychgate, I pause to read the Churchyard Rule's [sic]. They are exhaustive but impressively written in rain-affected, sepia ink. I gather that the ground must be kept flat as far as possible. No room for upstarts here! There is one gravestone that defies this commandment. It has outsize capitals! Another, still older, has only the words 'in memory of' – the rest erased by time. A young serviceman and an ATS girl from the village have standard, military-style stones which stand out, white and sensible, in the sun. There is a spreading beech near which, a marker says, twenty rose trees were planted in memory of a member of the Gregory family in 1956. There are lots of Tulls, calling 'Goodnight, God bless,' or other such poignant words after lights out, in spite of the 'rule's.'

I sit under the spreading beech to eat my lunch, dwelling on the problem of mortality. It is not surprising that elegies are best written in churchyards. All one can say at the end is that nature takes over: the trees flourish, making even the church itself look perishable. St Mary's, Aldermaston, is sickly pebbledashed; fine inside, I believe; but locked. So I must go back to the lively village which is for me an architectural feast. Ah, here is 5 Church Road, with its superscription Mannerley. Here is Sally-Anne, the maker of the patchwork quilt of *Memories* which has drawn me to this place. Here, too, are her three dogs, identical flat-coated retrievers 'We'll go for a walk in the park!' Now I shall see how the other half lives!

If, as my brother used to say, churchyards are the story books of England, then I say parklands are their bindings. And how is it that trees in a park are always so superior? Is it because they occupy so much space? Trees in a hundred acres grow better than trees in only ten; and trees in a thousand, still better, it seems. Of course plants like company; they thrive in colonies and dominions. They nourish one another with their droppings and enrich their successors by their own decay. Then parks – like the abbeys of old – enjoy the best alluvial sites. There is usually a river at hand or a mountain torrent to supply every kind of plant that a man might need. Look at those cedars! Look at that lake! Look at that complex – built by Blue Circle Cement after the atomic plant departed. (I keep these remarks to myself, being grateful to Sally-Anne for her intelligent insights and hospitality.)

Parts of the old house that replaced the original one that was burned down remain. The concrete wonder that stands by the lake – occupied this afternoon by a lone cormorant – looks what it is: a conference centre. What, one wonders, will it look like in years to come?

Aldermaston has the ability to accommodate artists and scientists, sportsmen, entrepreneurs, interlopers and tourists alike. And by some symbiotic miracle the real life of the village goes on. New people move in, but the old families remain. Sally-Anne's book is a testament to this. 'Change and Helping Others' is one headline, constantly echoed throughout this remarkable story of triumph over adversity. Sally-Anne is passionate about community – but so must most of these doughty villagers be.

Returning home with only the injured wheel of my bike in my hand – Sally-Anne has kindly conveyed me by car to the top of the ridge that separates the Kennet Valley from that of the Pang – I pick up a stout ash plant and march cheerfully downhill. The bells of Bucklebury church peal out: 'Come all to church, good people,' their notes spilling out over the

Swan at Aldermaston.

richly embroidered Sunday landscape. But it is still only about three in the afternoon. No doubt the resident ringers, or a visiting team, are practising their esoteric and peculiarly English art. They seem to me to gather together in one commingling all the bells I had ever heard: Ludlow, Canterbury and the bells of Old Bow. And, old farm lad that I am, one picture from Sally-Anne's book springs to mind: that of the cows in the 1960s meandering through the Street for milking, repeated in a tapestry by Effie Arlott – a member of one of the oldest families in the village. Threads drawn together, sealing for ever a moment in time.

The Greatest Little Theatre in the World

Is there a more out-of-the-way yet important theatre in the world than the Watermill? Stratford, Ontario, perhaps? I went there once, from Toronto, by bus, through little-known places with native American names, to the shore of Lake Huron, 150 miles, not to see a play but to hear Glenn Gould play the piano. (He had travelled about the same distance from Oshawa, I suppose.) I was piano-mad and homesick. I closed my eyes at Kitchener and Waterloo; but Stratford felt more like home. The audience was largely Colonial American, posh and opinionated; loud-voiced and well-dressed. Glenn sat low at his instrument, occasionally sipped water from a glass at the end of the keyboard but seemed, gently humming to himself, to be in a world of his own. So was I. It's not at all like that at the Watermill.

Founded about the same time, in the 1960s, the Watermill, near Newbury, is everything that one expects – but is still packed with surprises. It is cramped and intimate; it is bold and astonishing. It is what I suppose Elizabethan theatre was: darned uncomfortable – at least for the groundlings. It is high-risk, gambling on a shoe-string, still fighting for survival, ringing the changes between comedy, tragedy and farce, appealing for funds, reaching out to the schools and the wider community, performing in village halls, petitioning, propositioning and speaking up for itself. It is a raw heart left beating on the cold slab of this all-too digital world.

The Director's House, the Watermill Theatre.

A spectral millwheel sits in the tumbling waters of the Lambourn, visible through glass as you go in to the stalls. It looks like King Lear, cataracts and hurricanes spouting round its whitened, whiskery frame: all that is left of the machinery that drove this versatile nineteenth-century cornmill, successively used for fulling and fine paper-making before producing Restoration comedy, Shakespeare, vaudeville or what you will. It was started by the Gollins family in a wonderfully wacky way. (David Gollins originally thought of turning it into a cathedral!) Local actors – delighted to be indoors for a change – performed two plays in the summer. Then a man who was tired of London motored down and suggested he ran it for them. The man was a charlatan, decamped in debt, but left David determined to carry on. The story is legendary; there were no lavatories; the men used a cupboard by the millwheel; the bucket was emptied into the stream. The dressing rooms at the back of the stage were rudimentary. The first professional productions were directed by David Gilmore between 1976 and 1978. He writes in a memoir that he once sat at his desk watching a heron take a trout from the river only a few feet away; and on another occasion after the audience had all gone home a solitary nightingale sang fit to bust on a post outside his office.

Then came the revelatory, the legendary and – sadly now – the late Jill Fraser who brought the theatre to its present pre-eminent pitch. Productions now transfer to London and Broadway. The tiny Watermill at Bagnor, near Newbury, with its chalk stream fringed with cressbeds (and old roadside notices warning of SOFT VERGES and WATER BIRDS NESTING) is, thanks to Mrs Fraser, nationally and internationally known.

Internationally known, too – but not so frequented – is the Greek theatre in the grounds of Bradfield College. Its origins are equally worth recalling. The book to use is Vincent's 1907 *Highways and Byways of Berkshire*. A Wykehamist himself, Mr Vincent is strong on public schools and he quotes from the *History of Bradfield College* by Mr Arthur Leach, 'an authority of the highest order, a friend and connection of my own, and before this little book had been conceived, simply because, as our public schools are among the most distinct and characteristic of English institutions, so their development is, to one of the opinion just expressed, an absorbing story to read. . . . Stevens of Bradfield [the clerical founder] never counted the cost beforehand. . . . He was impelled by his own momentum; he would comfort an assistant master, whose salary had not been paid, by recommending him to repeat the Nicene Creed. . . . Before he died his manor and lands had been sold, his Rectory had been sequestrated . . .'

The school, we are told, was opened, with one boy, in February 1850. It passed through a long period of stress and storm and the man who was to save it appeared in the person of Dr Gray, an ardent Wykehamist, and scholar of Queen's College, Oxford. There is always a hero in good public school stories!

What struck Mr Vincent most, he says, on the day of his visit, was the excellent physique of the boys and their appearance of robust health. He comments on the pleasing buildings, the ancient wall of red brick, having – in 1907 – at one end the hexagonal chamber called Tom o' Bedlam's Hole, probably of fourteenth-century work. Very much more attractive, however, is the exact reproduction of a Greek theatre in a chalk pit adjoining the college, with a Greek Temple for stage building or scene. In it have been produced a long succession of Greek plays, causing the fame of Bradfield to go out all over the world.

CHAPTER FIVE

A Walk to Yattendon in Snow

Only three days later, I am walking to Yattendon – something I have done many times in the past seven years. It is a short walk between neighbouring villages; but in about 3 miles it encompasses almost everything that is essentially English. Even during the foot-and-mouth epidemic, the public footpaths through the surrounding beech woods remained open to walkers, provided dogs were kept on leads. The M4 booms monotonously, reminding one how miraculously we old codgers of Frilsham and Yattendon have been spared the worst scars of development that disfigure large areas of rural Berkshire. It is as if the motorway actually preserves our community, as it preserves the community of badgers that thrive in the setts abutting it.

Frilsham in the snow.

Frilsham Manor.

A week ago we, the old codgers and the badgers alike, were marvelling at the early appearance of bluebell shoots. Beeches were in bud; snowdrops and aconites were in bloom; hazel catkins were stretched to their fluorescent limit; and that most magical transformation, the bronzing of the willows by the river, was well under way. Today, the snow has totally transformed all that. The butterflies that last week wantoned in warm air have folded their wings and – one hopes – found shelter and gone back to sleep.

Now however, the hardy old codgers come into their own. On the second day of this unexpected cold snap, the snow on the woodland trails bears not only the prints of animals but those of humans as well. It is as if all those old cottagers of former days, the farm hands and the woodchoppers, the carters and clay-diggers, the keepers and poachers, have all been about. And yet I see no one. There is only the odd surprised pheasant. The most prominent tracks are those of foxes – more often smelt than seen round here. You would need to be David Attenborough and Conan Doyle to work out all the clues woven into this transient and timeless tapestry. Birds have done all the more fancy stitching; deer have left their double slots, dogs their heavy, rounded hind-pad marks; some of the finer fanned etchings may be the work of squirrels; but the badgers seem to have had a lazy night, bedded down in bracken in underground bunkers beneath old spoil-heaps of earth from the motorway, built four decades ago. The woods decay, adding to their stately pleasure domes of raised earth, fallen trees and spreading rhododendrons. The snow that makes all things new cancels concerns about the future and paradoxically brings into focus the past.

I first came this way – the dog tracks remind me – when the motorway was being built. Forty years and four dogs later, my clumsy footprints look the same. (Similarly, on sunny days, my dark-quiffed, straight-backed shadow marches agelessly beside or ahead of me.) Trees have fallen, but the woods remain. They constantly renew themselves. In the midst of death we are in life. I pick up the paper (headline: SNOW BRINGS MISERY TO MILLIONS) from the village stores, established 1877. About that date, a remarkable man, Alfred Waterhouse, having walked from Pangbourne station out to Yattendon, and been impressed by this wooded rump of land, possessed of abundant clay and timber, decided – being an architect – to build a new manor house which he

Yattendon Village Stores.

Frilsham Church.

called Yattendon Court. He and his friend Robert Bridges added soul to this foundation by extending the church, remodelling the village and giving the people of Yattendon not only employment but also arts and crafts to fill their leisure hours. What, I wonder, were the headlines in the papers in 1877? Reform was in the air. Disraeli had secured Suez and created his queen Empress of India; continuing confidence at home was based, as Asa Briggs has written, on economic strength and social balance. Certainly the headline writers in 1877 would have concerned themselves with weightier matters than a one-night fall of snow.

CHAPTER SIX

Civil War & Civil Disobedience

Dark clouds have always hung over these dumpy-looking foothills of the Downs. Berkshire has only one Civil War castle still standing; but what a story it tells! Donnington, just outside Newbury, was the site of an epic siege under the doughty royalist commander Sir John Boys. (Doughty is a word we shall use again and again in this account of the heroes – and heroines – of conflicts which with surprising regularity have erupted on the face of this small area of Berkshire earth.) It is most easily approached by a public footpath from the Blackbird Inn at Bagnor, or from Donnington village itself. Either way, paths run all around this most imposing relic of the Civil War. It is part of the greater landscape theatre of these parts.

Donnington Castle.

It is most impressive on a not-too-sunny day, when clouds lend a smoky blue-black drama and distance to the air. From Bagnor, you gain by seeing the A34 – an escape route which Sir John Boys could never have envisaged – and the Donnington Valley golf course in striking contrast to the battered shell of the gate-house, twin-towered and stiff-upper-lipped on the hill. The portcullis still bares its teeth. The flint earthworks still grin beyond the grassy ditch. The motte is still worth rolling down. But how, one always wonders, did Sir John, perched in his stone eyrie, hold out for twenty months? No doubt the round towers would help to deflect the Parliamentary cannon-balls; the apparently anti-clockwise stairways would force any rash invader to use his sword in his left hand; the magnificent keep would give the royalists a peerless view. My conclusion is that Sir John was simply well-provisioned; and unlucky that the Parliament forces chose ultimately to press home their advantage. For the Civil War was a long and tragic tale of waste on both sides; not only of men but of opportunities. The King was for ever repositioning himself; Sir John and his men beat off successive attacks; in 1646 Donnington, in military parlance, was 'relieved'. The irony now is that a man with no more claim to be a strategist than an occasional golfer can freely view the castle from all sides and marvel at its commanding position and its endurance – but equally at its unhappy fate.

Newbury owes its war- (and peace-) time importance to its position at the crossing of east–west and north–south routes. Everywhere one goes in west Berkshire one is reminded of this. It would be instructive, but exhausting, to visit all the places in the neighbourhood associated with the Civil War. Mention must be made of the Falkland Memorial – as strange and melodramatic a monument as any I have seen. It commemorates those who fell in the first battle of Newbury, 1643; in particular, the King's right-hand man, his Secretary of State, Viscount Falkland, as big a hero as you will come across in any day's march.

Fine weather and an easy ride are in prospect for me the next day. Fortified with an orange, some honey, cod-liver oil and blood-pressure tablets that Captain Cook would have scorned, I stow the bike in the back of the car and prepare to circumnavigate Newbury – as large an obstacle to my passage in the early morning as Australia. I can take the eastern passage through Thatcham and Greenham; or I can take the western one through Enborne and Skinners Green – as bloody a battle scene as any in the Civil War. Once I reach the canal on either side, I can glide along on my bicycle with no care in the world. (Where to leave the car remains a problem, however, as it always will be.) The Robin Hood roundabout forces me into a decision. I go west.

The Hungerford stretch of the A4, the old Bath road, would be easy to cycle along, being mostly downhill; but here the early morning traffic is intense –

Avington church.

though not so horrific as on the Basingstoke, Winchester and Andover routes. Kintbury lies along here, down by the canal; a pleasant spot; but not so inviting as Avington – and still not too far from my goal.

Avington – or Avalon? After the rough and tumble of modern Newbury, this place shines like a good deed in a naughty world. Or, rather, like a well-kept secret in a rowdy and uncivil one.

There is a short, straight avenue of interesting hardwoods leading downhill to white gates at the end, denoting an estate. A notice states that the grounds inside the gates are private but that visitors to the church are welcome and that the key may be obtained from the first of the four cottages. Greensward sweeps down to the river, sprinkled with snowdrops. A huge cedar tree dominates the churchyard, throwing a protective arm over what Simon

The interior of Avington church.

Jenkins calls the most complete Norman church in Berkshire. To one side are typical Berkshire red brick-and-tile farm buildings, grouped behind a flint-walled manor house. The apex of one of these buildings is surmounted with a weathervane, crowned by a horse. The clean and tidy orderliness of everything, the straight post and rail fencing running everywhere and the covey of spindly-legged yearlings out grazing in one of the paddocks denote a rather special racing establishment. But this is all private; the church, the trees and the green grass stretching down to the river and its consort the canal interest me. I ask the lady at the cottage with the key where I may safely leave my car. 'Inside the gates,' she says, surprisingly. 'Just drive up; they'll open.' They do. The Normans had no such defence.

Presently I am photographing the scene, the huge metal key hung in the pocket of my fleece. I move on, still marvelling at my good fortune, towards the church and realise that, somewhere in all that grass, I have dropped the key. I retreat to the spot where I took the last photograph, where – I carefully worked out – the river and canal are seen to best advantage. I circumnavigate that spot a hundred times in ever-widening circles of despair. How can I be such a fool? How can I lose a key so large? I hope no one can see me stupidly treading and retreading this same small patch of ground. A man drives out from the farm with a tractor along the track to the fields. I half hope he doesn't see me. He drives back. Drives out again. Attending to the horses, no doubt. I am in tears and on the point of giving up my search. A thousand years of church-going at Avington halted by me losing the key! In desperation I signal to the man. He stops, dismounts from the tractor and comes over to me. 'We'll find it,' he says comfortingly. 'In a hundred years, perhaps – or a horse will tap it with its shoe tomorrow' He is a handsome, well-balanced lad.

Completely untroubled by the loss of a key. 'Many worse things in the world – worse luck!' He strides purposefully about the grass while I crumple up. 'You sure you didn't leave it in the car?' He checks all possibilities. I assure him that it was here where I took the photograph that I must have dropped it. He is sure we would see it if it were. His strides have taken him almost to the church door, into the shade of the trees. A long triumphant arm goes up. From this distance I cannot see the smile – I cannot see the key; but I know he has found it.

The site of the lost key.

My adventures after that are an anticlimax: a quick look round the church with its small, round-headed windows, its ancient, sagging chancel arch, its baffling font with images of the devil, a bishop and (possibly) Judas kissing Christ, and its grizzled, iron-hard door which, after admitting pilgrims for a thousand years, still jibs at the turn of the key; and, after that, a short spin along the canal on my bike. I will have to leave the Falkland Memorial for another day; all I can think of now is the horseman's kindness and my hope that, if any bedraggled Civil War soldier on his way to or from Newbury passed this place, he felt its peace.

And so to Greenham, for ever associated with war and rumours of war. In fact this part of Berkshire – perhaps the first to be settled by foreign invaders – might be called the cockpit of the south. One thinks of Alfred footing it to Reading to treat with Guthrum, while still trying to organise resistance to the Danes behind his back in the wetlands of Somerset. These gravelly hollows and gorse-clad humps around Greenham Common must have always harboured snipers and spies. Yet the village itself has a great history. It was part of the Preceptory of Knights Hospitallers established in the reign of Henry II. In 1811, Greenham Mill was owned by John Coxeter who, having introduced machinery into his mill, boasted that he could take the coat off his friend Sir John Throckmorton's back, reduce it to wool, and within twenty-four hours turn it back into a coat again. Hence the famous Newbury Coat. Greenham has always brought credit to the town of Newbury and is today a thriving arts centre.

The market place, Newbury.

Mention Newbury to someone who doesn't live here – may never have been here – and they say: 'Bypass . . . Racing . . . Vodafone . . .Greenham . . .' Its position at the crossroads – east–west, north–south – has inevitably given it an unfortunate reputation; but, pop a pin in the map, anywhere south or north of Newbury, and you will find a beacon or a royal hunting ground. It is a region like Kipling's part of Sussex, full of 'stilly woods' and 'dimpled tracks.' I begin to realise that this is no common earth through which the Kennet flows; but it was only a matter of time before COMMUNICATION, for which Newbury seems to have been born, would awaken this sleepy market town to her true destiny. Her fairy godmothers, however, have not all been good fairies, as we shall see.

✳   ✳   ✳

Still, one needs to be cautious. How different is modern Thatcham from its Mesolithic past! But one can still see the reed beds on the margins of the river where, perhaps 6,000 years BC, the first boat people from Europe bent branches of willow to frame their reed huts. The Greenham peace women simply telescoped 8,000 years when they used 'benders' to make their tents. With thoughts like this in mind, I approach Greenham and Aldermaston, trying to jettison preconceived notions, paring away prejudice and calluses grown over time.

Greenham, to start off with (as schoolboys used to say, with added emphasis), is a great place to cycle round; so, on a crisp February morning, I nose-dive out of Frilsham, down Hawkridge, up to Grimsbury Castle – hill fort, a mere 800 years BC – through Cold Ash – where Civil War names crop up, like Edgehill Close and Waller Drive – past Downe House (one of Berkshire's best known public schools), past Wood Leaves where Alec McCurdy makes fine furniture and musical instruments, out towards Reading, past the little stone chapel that used to be the Blue Coat School but has long been left like a poor child by the roadside, disregarded by the multitude of motorists who flash by on the A4. Sharp right for Crookham, says the sign, over the railway, canal and river and right again up Bury's Bank to Greenham. Simple!

The airfield stretches away to the left as you glide along past gorse bushes – always, it seems, in flower – birch trees hiding cottages or small-holdings tucked away to your right, notices warning of (unseen) horse-drawn vehicles and animals, cattle-grids and speed limits, gravelly pull-ins and innumerable public footpath signs. To the south are the smoky Hampshire hills and to the north the rolling Berkshire Downs. There are long sheets of water, like lakes over the length of the ridge. The odd wind-lashed pine. Take away the cars which use this road as a rat-run, and you could fancy you were in remote Ontario.

The Falkland Memorial.

You come down to earth in Pinchington Lane, where the people of West Berkshire dump their waste. (The extraction of gravel has left a sizable hole to be filled.) There is a sand and gravel company nearby offering building materials and landscape products to new house buyers. Houses here are packed in, not tucked away. Roundabouts abound. Eventually, by blundering on in true Civil War fashion, you come to the Falkland Memorial. It, too, seems diminished, side-lined and disregarded. It is also dwarfed by a giant cedar tree nearby. A boy on half-term holiday from school is seated at the top of the steps that form the base of the obelisk. He is absorbed with his mobile phone. I squint to read the lettering which, though carved in granite, is growing faint: LUCIUS CARY, VISCOUNT FALKLAND, AGED 32. That much I can pick out. Then on one side there is a quotation from Thucydidides; on another, one from Livy; and, on another, one from Burke: THE BLOOD OF MAN IS WELL SHED FOR OUR FAMILY, FOR OUR FRIENDS, FOR OUR GOD, FOR OUR COUNTRY, FOR OUR KIND. THE REST IS VANITY. THE REST IS CRIME.

I wonder if the boy makes much of these sentiments. Does he know that, just up the road from here in Skinners Lane, the dead bodies of horses and men so filled the lane that the wounded could not be brought to the surgeons in town?

Returning through Greenham village, I marvel at the apparent ease with which it has recovered from the scars of the Cold War; how the open common land has returned to its eerie, natural calm. It seems like an oasis of peace. If so, those despised women – thought and spoken of as witches, harlots and lesbians – who broke through the perimeter fence, then symbolically repaired it with wool, achieved more with their weaving of fragile strands into webs of ever greater strength than the men of the Civil War who so needlessly – but heroically – fought each other and shed each other's blood.

It is with relief that we leave this theatre of war and head for the peace of the downs. East Hendred is, by all accounts, one of the prettiest villages in Berkshire and one I have never seen. We may go by Compton and Applepie Hill, head up to the Ridgeway, then bowl along westward as far as Scutchamer Knob, avoid Harwell (we have had enough of atomic establishments) and at last gain the minor road north to the village. These little roads are coloured primrose yellow on my Landranger map but, like primroses, are not always easy to find. It is a long old way and we may find ourselves panting for breath.

No hill in old or new Berkshire is more than 300 metres above sea level. Scutchamer Knob is only 203. But the lie of the land here is altogether different from that of the south. Yes, the Ridgeway runs west to east, as do the ridges of the south. Berkshire, it seems, rose from her Pliocene sea-bed, leaving a coverlet of chalk, creased this way and that but mostly downwards and printed all over with whorls of wide or narrow contour lines, green beech-groves and gallops whose turf was made specially for horses. The same turf, bitten down by sheep over centuries and springy with thyme, is especially good for walking on.

Come, we have been seduced, carried away; we are like public schoolboys AWOL ,out of bounds, but enjoying breaking the rules set by our local administrators. Besides. East Hendred will be good for our souls. After all, Falkland, Skinners Green, Greenham and even AWE at Aldermaston have almost faded out of mind, as if they had never been; but East Hendred, the books say, is wholesomely full of its living past. 'With its Manor House in the heart of the village . . . streets that have ancient names, the virgate of land that is still called Paternoster, grass terraces testifying to the linen industry of days gone by, its half-ruined chapel of the Carthusians, its grand Anglican church, and "Elizabethan farmhouse" (once doubtless occupied by Benedictine monks and farmers) and a modern Roman Catholic chapel in pure and severe Gothic, East Hendred is a village of no ordinary attraction to the mere passer-by.' We have Mr Vincent's word for it. Once a centre for the wool trade, it was starved, he says, by James I, who desired to encourage Ilsley – where we will go later. Mr Vincent was writing in 1907; but I am sure some of what he marvelled at will still be there; and who can resist a virgate of land – something that has existed since Domesday? Come!

* * *

On 26 February Providence intervenes – Providence in her bad fairy guise. Bad weather and my wife's illness force me to become domesticated. February is never a good month for small, grey animals like me. It may be short, but it is almost unendurable. It really tests your strength. What is a poor biped to do?

Yattendon church.

One's cycle is unreliable. You say 'Buck up, Ariel!' but it seems not to recognise its new name and stands moping in the shed, its tyres not wholly flat but not encouragingly firm either. Then, out of the blue, comes one fine day – the only one of the week, the forecasters say. This little furry thing turns Toad, gets in his motor car and says 'Poop!' to pedalling or footing it and goes purring round his local estate. After all, one can be too much seduced by foreign travel and neglect one's own affairs.

Frilsham is really part of Yaddendon estate, owned by Lord Iliffe – an estate which extends to Aldworth and beyond. There are other smaller units of land, but Yattendon is the only large estate in the area which has remained intact – a surprising success in the light of today's agricultural difficulties, and a story in itself. Alfred Waterhouse would have been proud of it. From that small acorn that he planted in 1876 a great, enduring oak has sprung.

My first call is Yattendon School which the visionary Waterhouse built himself. Can I believe my luck? The children are out in a sunlit group, smiling

Yattendon school.

at their teachers who are taking photographs of them. Click, I snap them, too; then ask if they mind. 'Of course not!' Everyone is happy – not least the children. They and their teachers are an advertisement for good, old-fashioned country schools. Bully for 1876, I say!

Just down the road, is the turn for Stanford Dingley. You cannot resist Stanford Dingley and its church when the sun and snowdrops are out; crocuses, too; and the odd intrepid daffodil! What is even more surprising is

Stanford Dingley church.

that the church is open. On a Monday! And that the notes for visitors are actually clear and comprehensive. One item particularly attracts my attention: 'The coat of arms above the chancel is very rare . . . It was stolen from the church in 1976. The local residents were discussing its theft in the Bull shortly afterwards and a woman who overheard the conversation said she had seen something like it in an antique shop in Twickenham the day before. Incredibly, it was the same one. It has now been fastened slightly higher up the wall!'

The church is strikingly, almost startlingly, beautiful outside. Its white, wooden bell tower soars among trees, almost piercing the high cumulus on this sun-bright, happy day. You have to back into a hedge to try to photograph it without losing the weather vane which is lost anyway among the topmost twigs. Nothing but a tractor rumbles by, taking FYM out to the fields. Only yesterday, I read that green woodpeckers – prevalent in our area – were formerly persecuted for boring holes in the shingles of such steeples. Luckily, our green woodpeckers and steeples cohabit and survive.

I am off to Aldworth, via Ashampstead's woody lanes, where – unless you are unlucky – you will hardly see a house. Yes, there is the old thatched

Aldworth church.

The interior of Aldworth church.

coaching inn called Four Points. Then a cottage where you suddenly turn left to the church, almost wholly hidden from the world by the hump of ground under which it stands, shielded and remarkably preserved. It has no steeple; it has hardly a tower; it has, instead a sort of monk's hood which is orange in the sun. Aldworth is in all the books, famous for its de la Beche giants. Unlike Stanford Dingley – too pretty, perhaps, for the academic connoisseur – it does not have such intimate memorials as the little brass plate which honours one E.C. Grace, Warden from 1895 to 1945. Instead we have these lumbering giants in effigy beside the walls and between the aisles, prostrate in armour, crowding out the congregation – yet, by their comatose barbarity, bestowing peace. One, too terrible in life, is laid somewhere outside, under the west wall of the church. More redemptive, to my mind, is the tapestry done to mark the millennium by some ladies of the village which hangs inside, though it may not endure so long as the tombs.

Outside in the sun again, I wander down a lane to Dumworth Farm, which is a world apart. The house is clearly grand – and the barns behind perhaps older and grander still. This 'backside' of Aldworth is so hidden away, it must be worth investigating. Yes, this – not the domain of the doomed de la Beche family – is more to my liking. Barns – not one or two but a collection of them

– inhabit the walled expanse of land behind the house. Their roofs are long and steep, black as pitch and wonderfully preserved. They are almost impossible to photograph, but delightful to sketch. My immediate response to barns such as these though is to people them in my imagination with tousled farm-workers, bustling in and out of their great double doors, calling 'Whoa!' to their horses and steadying before emptying the swaying wagons of corn. Almost 300 years of rural history is here intact, sleeping, maybe, like the giants in the church, but symbolic of the very Bread of Life on which not only the prosperity of England but the wealth of other nations was built, endorsed and enduring, not destructive and dead. Sticking my chest out with pride and armed with my sketch-pad, I knock on the door of the house. A scrabble of lion-hearted terriers; a scuffle of keys. The glass in the door reveals a lady dressed to go out. I try to escape, ashamed of the trouble I am causing. I signal my retreat but the lady opens the door and welcomes me in. I stutter something about barns, making her wonder perhaps whether I want to buy one. 'You need to see my husband.' Deservedly, I am left with the dogs – but not for long. Husband proves to be even more enthusiastic about barns – and certainly more knowledgeable - than I. 'The big one is 1748. You know the game we used to play trying to see how much we could throw over our

Dumworth Farm barns.

shoulder?' He is testing me, to see if I really am a farmer's son – if I really know what I'm talking about when it comes to barns. I hum and ha a while. 'I did a bit of pitching when I was a boy.' 'That's it! To get the last load up into the top of the barn you had to toss it over the bar.' 'I don't remember a bar. We used to pitch to a man half way up in a well, then he'd pitch the sheaf on up to the man on top, squashed under the roof. Hot as hell! And dark!' We are like a couple of kids. His wife goes out and leaves us to it.

'Now this house. You see this porch. How old do you think it is?' He is testing me again. I compare the brickwork with that of the rest of the house, which is clearly Georgian. It could be newer. It could be older. I plump – because I am never right in these matters – for the latter. 'Wrong!'

He draws my attention to one pane of old glass in the sash windows in the main front of the house. 'How do you know?' I ask. 'By the reflection.' Peering more carefully, I can see that it is darker. I am learning, but I still see through a glass darkly. . . .

This gentleman is surprisingly tolerant of my ignorance. He has obviously both the enthusiasm for history and the training that I lack. He is going to see me again, when the weather outlook is better – possibly next week. 'Range around and sketch as much as you like. Better knock on the door though when you come. I have closed-circuit television in my office. I see everyone who's about!' I pat the old moss-encrusted gate as I leave. I have found a kindred spirit in a kindred world.

Returning home by Wyld Court, I notice the RDA stables. Stables interest me, draw me – like barns. I wander in. Two ladies and a gentleman advance with wheelbarrows with the usual cargo, bedding or fodder or manure. I give the usual vague account of myself. 'Mr Davies is an artist,' one says. 'Then he'll do us a picture to be auctioned in May, for funds for the association,' says the other lady who is, I understand, chairman of the Riding for the Disabled, Newbury Group.

'But how do you know me?' I ask the first lady. 'I introduced you to my husband at the farm, just now,' she says. I stutter my apologies, promising to do a picture – and it had better be good, I tell myself!

Nothing is more stimulating to a writer than the chance to observe in the way an artist observes. It isn't until you have set yourself up, chosen the angle from which best to view the subject and pondered the palaver of perspective and scale that you realise how very little we harassed twentieth-century people even think about such things. Chuffed with my afternoon's harvest, I decide next morning to add to my load. I call at Hawkridge Farm where the house is even earlier than Dumworth. It is sixteenth-century, has geese on a pond, fantails on the dovecote, a well-house, a laundry, a long covered way, linking other buildings in that sensible, practical way that our forefathers had of

One of the horses at the stables.

gathering units together as it were in a courtyard, combining elegance with considerations of safety and convenience. And, of course, there is the great barn whose roof is so long and steep that it is now covered with thousands of small, locally-made tiles but was obviously originally thatched. Mr Meadows, the owner, is just as informative about dates. I plead shortage of time – and sun. 'Come any time! I'll warn my wife! Summer's the best time, when the half-timbering on the front of the house' – which is double-crucked but north-facing – 'gets the sun.' So I have an assignment for the summer, as well. But I think I shall be back there in a week.

East Hendred, Sans Pareil

Best Kept Village in Berkshire 1973, Best Kept village in Oxfordshire, 1974, says the brass plate on Champs Chapel – now the museum, unfortunately only open for further information on the first Sunday afternoon of the month. In other words, look and see for yourself. East Hendred, you soon realise, is exclusive and exceptional, and must have long since fought off any competitors for the title of Best Kept Village, whether in Berkshire or Oxfordshire – or in England, come to that. It has 'Estate Village' written all over it. Kings Manor, right there in the centre of the village is downright, royally monastic. Stout walls and heavy oak doors shut the peripatetic out. I try the heavy, lion-headed, iron handles of one in vain. A man drives up with a van bearing scaffolding, opens it with ease and invites me in. 'Old,' I mouth on the cobbles. 'A bit,' he agrees. I'll see if there's anybody in . . .' There is no answer, so I have the outer courtyard to my amazed self, while he, too busy to stand around, mounts like a cat to the high roof of the house and calls to someone at a house on the other side for a cup of tea: two sugars, please.

Leaving Kings Manor, with its great thatched barn and walls curving away in the direction of Oxford, I head west down the High Street, past houses and barns of every style of architecture, the Eyston Arms (one of many pubs), a house called Dancing Hill, the half-timbered, herring-boned Wisteria House – and post office – till I reach the Old Estate Yard – where is the Estate Office? – and a walk southward to woods which I take to be the famous virgate of land. The view over to the church, however, tempts me back to the village. There is nowhere like a churchyard, especially if it has table tombs, for a nice noon lunch, al fresco and free.

On my way, a youth, pimply and pale, who could not climb onto a pogo-stick, informs me that Dancing Hill may have been a church. There is a private Catholic chapel in the manor grounds; there appears to be a church of St Mary as well as this the parish church of St Augustine of Canterbury. So how many churches are there altogether? As many as there are pubs, I conclude – still resisting the temptation to go into one, on such a beautiful day. My new friend informs me that he has lived in East Hendred for two years and he still hasn't seen it all.

The path to the west door of the church has an avenue of yews, trimmed like those at Painswick: the twelve apostles, I suppose. Chimes accompany the striking of the hour in the tower. I marvel at the Old Cottage – which really merits the name – with its high, thatched wall by the roadside; Croft Barn with its bowed roof and Church Cottage with its galvanised dustbins – looking strangely antiquated to our 'green' eyes. But I am soaked with sun and saturated with six centuries of prime preservation by these Eystons, whose property – one hopes – East Hendred may long continue to be!

✳   ✳   ✳

A ridge of high pressure sits slap bang on top of us bringing with it a warm wind from the Azores. Eighty years and seven days precisely, I consider myself not too old to tackle Inkpen Beacon and Walbury Hill's near-mountainous height (just under 1,000ft, that is.) Terry at Avington tells me I cannot get through from there.

'Not even on foot?'

'Not even on foot!' These horsemen are hard, so I leave the car at Lower Denford, near Hungerford; eject Ariel from his lodging in the boot; mount and follow the avenue of sycamores over Hungerford Common. So dazzled by sunlight am I that I miss the Inkpen Gate and head for Templeton, which turns out to be a gain because I see mares and foals – besides all the other signs of spring – and a grand house with gardens and glass houses stretching for hundreds of yards beyond. (It is a very ugly grand house – obviously nineteenth-century and thoroughly unsuitable for what passes for fast rather than easy living now.) There is no sign of life except the chink of a shovel on gravel behind South Lodge. I peer round the back, where an abyss of chalk opens up with a single soul laying what appear to be the foundations of an extension.

'What is the big house called?' I ask.

'House Hydro,' he seems to say. 'It's going to be turned into flats.' He doesn't deal in details, this man, so I leave him to his footings with a puzzled 'Thanks!' A brief look at my map as I sit on a bank of wide-awake celandines suggests it is Totterdown House. There is one white mare and her dark foal in a paddock simply inviting a photograph, the foal full of inquisitiveness and banishing all thoughts of splendours of the past. The world is new-minted for him. He reels round his dam in ever-widening circles, exploring the size of everything – including his strength. And his speed! It is greater than mine. Inkpen is still 3 miles. And the hill is another 3 beyond.

In the village, I find a man mending his fence. He is ready for a cup of coffee, he says; would I like one, too? His turns out to be the sixteenth-century thatched cottage that John Schlesinger used in the film, *Black Legend*, telling the story of George Broomham and Dorothy Newman who were hanged on Coombe Gibbet for the murder his wife and child in the reign of Charles II. Would I like to see the church? Raa-ther! And, of course, the old rectory and the huddle of cottages around. Then, with a last slaver of civilised conversation for a while, I go on to study the hill and its only occupants this lovely day – the sheep.

Bridgeman's, Inkpen.

I suddenly realise that I haven't seen a car for miles: only the long, winding, narrow, uphill road. 'Public Footpath,' says a sign, which I take to be a short cut to the top. With Ariel abandoned in what is left of a hedge, I continue on foot. It reminds of Pontesford Hill in Shropshire, similarly scalped by wind. Taxingly steep. Turf springy from being trodden for a thousand years by many thousands of sheep. Today, there are only about a hundred on the far – the south – side of the hill. They are hardy and horned with a good admixture of Scottish Blackface in their blood. A few plastic bottles denote the recent presence of Man. The gibbet – the fifth replacement, heavily reinforced on all sides with steel – is scrawled with illegible tokens of love, perhaps as a last resort. The sky is summer-blue. The gate reserved for use by TVHG club members is left open, so I take an even shorter – and steeper – cut down to rejoin my bike. My eyes open to the geology of the vale – mainly by a huge swathe of newly ploughed chalk – I bowl down the Hungerford road like a visiting angel, glowing at the sight of earth's innocence and beauty – and none of its stains on my wings.

Hungerford Common, with its beautiful avenues of trees and wide acres of grass, is a well-ordered public place. 'Welcome,' a notice says, 'to Open Access Land to enjoy the countryside, see animals and watch birds.' I do not offend by 'Driving Vehicles, Horse Riding, Camping, Hang-Gliding, Paragliding,

CHAPTER SEVEN

Hamstead Marshall

The Cloud-Capped Towers & Gorgeous Palaces

This, our latest port of call on the canal – the Navigation as it was known – is the archetypal Lost Domain. Enchantment and heartache abound here. It calls to mind almost everything one remembers best in Romantic poetry: 'Tread softly because you tread on my dreams . . . Our sweetest songs are those that tell of saddest thought . . . Darkling I listen (for in these canal-side thickets one may yet hear the nightingale) . . . Charmed magic casements, opening on the foam (the river racing over the weir) . . . in

Gate pillars at Hamstead Marshall.

Church Cottage, West Hanney.

The Plough at West Hanney.

A Lambourn farmhouse.

Cottage at Bucklebury.

Cottages at Donnington.

The gibbet on Inkpen Beacon.

Ballooning, or Using a Metal Detector,' while I am there; and I am glad to see that Golfing is ruled out, too. But I am also glad to stow my virtuous bike in the back of the car and drive full-throttle home!

Now, I kid myself, I only have to 'loop the loop' round the Ridgeway, the Lambourn Valley – my favourite – and bowl along the Kennet and Avon Canal. Such is the effect of a perfect spring day on eighty-year-old legs.

fairy lands forlorn. Forlorn! The very word is like a bell . . . Fled is that music: Do I wake or sleep?' Yeats, Shelley and Keats might all have drawn inspiration from this place. Indeed, it is not just a lost domain; it is a lost empire; a lost world. We can count ourselves lucky to go there on this visit to the Kennet and Avon Canal.

It is midway between Newbury and Kintbury, just to the left of Avington – with which it shares a magical Camelot charm, like that of an old aquatint. You leave the busy Bath road behind and enter a world apart; a world of secrets only gradually revealed. For, under the smoothed surface of this prime riverside land there are many layers; the smoothing has gone on over many, many years.

We first hear of Hamstead Marshall as the home of William, Earl Marshal of England in the thirteenth century, famously celebrated in a poem entitled 'Histoire de Guillaume le Mareschal'. He served under Henry II, Richard the Lionheart, King John and the child Henry III, to whom he was regent. He must have been the most powerful commoner in England, the owner of more than one great estates. He died at his manor house in Caversham, Reading, and is commemorated in the Temple church in London. His son married Henry III's sister, Eleanor. The king made a grant of twenty does to William, Junior, for the park at Hamstead – our Berkshire woods being then just an extension of the royal forest at Windsor. But, it is to be supposed, there was only a collection of mud cottages grouped around a Norman church above the river at this time. Much was to change.

Onto this expansive, open stage in the early seventeenth century stepped William, 1st Earl of Craven, favourite of Charles I and lover of the king's sister, to whom he may even have been secretly married. The Craven family amassed estates in several counties of England. It looked as if their mansion at Hamstead would be the finest of all. But the hapless William, married or not, died childless. A number of Williams inherited Hamstead, but in 1718 the mansion was burned to the ground and the estates passed to one Fulwar Craven, a field sportsman and founder of the famous Craven Hunt. After some attempts to rebuild the original house, it is believed that the present Regency style mansion was an adaptation of a former hunting lodge. Fulwar was succeeded by another William who, like so many of the family, died childless. In 1767, the sixth baron – another William – married Elizabeth, a notable beauty who left her husband to his country pursuits and took to travelling abroad where she met the Margrave of Anspach, ruler of a small German principality. Both her husband and the Margrave's wife died conveniently within a short space of time and Elizabeth returned to her estates in Berkshire as the Margravine of Anspach, disapproved of by the most elevated in society but content to write plays which she produced and acted in

*Beeches in the park at
Hamstead Marshall.*

both in London and at home. She died in Naples and is buried in the English
cemetery there.

   The earldom – as distinct from the baronry – was revived at the end of the
eighteenth century. The new earl, a military man, married an actress, Louisa,
who, when he died, left her £15,000 a year. But money, as has been frequently
observed, cannot buy happiness. The Napoleonic Wars badly affected
England's rural economy; there were machine riots in 1830; the new Lord
Craven met Charles Dundas at Kintbury and raised the militia to combat the
mob. One man was hanged. Whatever else the Cravens had, they had
uncommon bad luck. One earl shot himself in 1983, aged twenty-six. In 1990
another earl died in a car crash and Hamstead Park passed from the Craven
family into other hands.

You are, by now, familiar with the canal on which the Margravine poetically expatiated under the name: The Navigation. Nothing prepares you, however, for the surprises that await you at the top of the hill, where stands the church. It is a fairly ordinary-looking church. Square, but not even in the way that some dancing is square. You step inside the graveyard, though, and there to your right is a saturnine figure bending at a tomb: a tramp, perhaps, eating his breakfast? It has a hideous, heavy, Victorian- gothic, look. You cross over to it and you see that it is someone's morbid idea of an angel with something like a sheaf of flowers – lilies, perhaps – in its hand. It is dated 1919. The name FRANCIS DE MURRIETA appears on the tomb.

The church is disappointingly locked. It might be better, you suppose, inside than out. You read all about it in the porch. Edward III visited in the mid-fourteenth century and may have entered through the Norman-arched doorway. William Craven, it says, began his house in 1661, initially as a palace for his beloved Elizabeth Stuart, exiled Queen of Bohemia, but she died soon after. It was planned to resemble a Heidelberg Palace by the architect, Balthazar Gerbia, who died on site and is buried here. You imagine poor, celibate William pondering his fate in this place. His heart is not in it. By 1813, it says, the intended Heidelberg Palace was completely demolished and the Craven family moved to another site in the park.

So, let's see this park; our eyes have been drawn to it all along. There are walls everywhere – enough, it seems, to encompass the earth. And how many pairs of ornamental gate-piers are there: two, four, six or eight? They rise up everywhere, topped by fantastical balls or cornucopias or emblems of fertility – you don't know what to call them. Aristos with knobs on, you think. And the trees are like the trees in parks everywhere – whether from special planting of favoured specimens or simply because they grow so companionably in a favoured place. There are yews, cedars, oaks, wellingtonias, beech, cherry and sycamore, mostly in bloom, all scenting the air. Those that grow by the river simply reach for the sky. The public footpaths lead in every direction, mostly on a made road. No cycles are permitted; so you walk.

You walk by the canal, too, for old time's sake. Memories are made of this – the water sloshing out of the lock-gates and sluices – and later over the weir, near where our little dachshund once fell in and I scooped her out with one hand like wet rabbit. You photograph the weir, revelling in the sunlight – as the salmon must revel in the ladder specially provided for them to return to their birthplace and die. 'Fallen Angel', a cabin cruiser, rests at her mooring, sad, empty and still. 'Inkie and I', a bustling narrowboat, goes by. Her captain hails 'Good morning!' A cloud of poplar cotton like soap-flakes blows in his face. Hawthorn buds look like beads of milk. Comfrey is beginning to flower, blue, pink and white. It is a perfect day. You feel like walking the circumference of the park.

The weir.

It is certainly beguiling enough, this park. How many acres? Several hundred, no doubt. There is the odd shell-shocked tree – its trunk hollowed out, but still bravely branching and leafing out above. There is the occasional complete fatality, the whitened corpse of a sycamore, the sturdy old body of an oak. Sheep and cattle graze, indifferent to their human connections. There is much replanting going on. But there is no one about. The silence is enormous. Only the cuckoo faintly breaks in from down by Kintbury perhaps, troubling the reed warblers in the sedges by the river there. Wouldn't you be bored by all this space, if you had to live here, every day? But, once in a while, it is heaven. Until you realise you may not be going in a circle, but veering out to the east – to Enborne and Newbury, in fact. Church Farm is just over the road.

A man tells you, yes, it is right for the church – but you don't want *that* church. You had better double back. No more trial and error now . . .

It is still beguiling, however, this expansive, open park – even without its Heidelberg Palace. You spot, this time round, the Regency replacement. And a stone with a plaque commemorating members of the American 501st Parachute Regiment who set up camp here in the war in preparation for the D-Day landings and returned from Normandy in the summer of 1944 before going to Holland in September to help liberate Europe. Geronimo and a bald eagle are emblazoned on the plaque. Eureka – and Geronimo, the bike is still where you left it! My patient, dainty Ariel! My diligence! My chick!

These words of Prospero's seem most apt at this point:

> Our revels now are ended. These our actors,
> As I foretold you, were all spirits and
> Are melted into air, into this air;
> And, like the baseless fabric of this vision,
> The cloud-capped towers, the gorgeous palaces,
> The solemn temples, the great globe itself,
> Yea, all which it inherit, shall dissolve;
> And, like this insubstantial pageant faded,
> Leave not a rack behind.

But Tennyson breaks in again at sight of willows, aspens and the island by the river . . . and I think of the beautiful, wayward Lady Craven, the Margravine, no longer trapped in her towered Camelot; I see her come down, find a boat beneath a willow left afloat . . . and, in true dream fashion, fulfil her destiny: 'she loosed the chain, and down she lay; the broad stream bore her far away . . .'

CHAPTER EIGHT

The Museum

In between jaunts, we rest. You cannot be jaunting all the time. A rolling stone gathers no moss. The place to gather moss is a museum. We have a particularly good one in Newbury, housed in the Jacobean Cloth Hall by the wharf and therefore near the Kennet and Avon Canal; but the towpath is not easily accessible from Frilsham, so I take the Long Lane route into town.

'I used to do that once,' shouts David, my neighbour, over the garden hedge.

'I do it twice,' I quip. 'There and back!' And, in spite of the traffic on our narrow roads, I find myself singing: 'The twenty-fifth of April two thousand and seven and I cycle like I'm only a schoolboy of eleven!' I surprise myself by my use of like for as – and the rhyme – but I shall be pleased to reach the safety of the cosy little Cloth Hall, where, I persuade myself that all the byways of Berkshire will be gathered into one.

The Old Cloth Hall in Newbury.

And so they are. It is a model of a museum in its setting, scope and presentation. Just now the *Daily Telegraph* is whipping up a storm about entrance fees at our cathedrals and inviting us to have our say: 'Tell us your church and museum rip-off stories.' Well, we in Berkshire have no cathedrals and I have come across no charges in churches I have visited – and our precious little museum is free.

The welcome is special. An old oil painting of the building in the reception area immediately catches your eye. A carter's horse and dray drawn alongside and a barge moored at the quay are just sufficient to give it scale and atmosphere. The building itself is boldly, if a little sketchily represented. A triumph! And, like so many of Berkshire's beauties, anonymous.

There, among the first and earliest exhibits, is the straight-toothed elephant's tusk – 2 metres long, found in the bed of the Kennet near Northbrook Street in 1887. Old straight-tooth lived in forests in milder periods of the Ice Age, we are informed. That sets you back on your heels! A million years, perhaps? European man introduced himself only 500,000 years ago. The cases of stuffed birds and mammals – a fox and a badger – I pass by. They are the all-too-familiar stuff of museums of my childhood. And the Roman coins. And the flint axe-heads and exhumed Stone Age bones. There is a handsome Bronze Age cremation urn from Brimpton which takes my eye, but proves to be only a copy of the real, fragmented thing. There is a marvellous portrait of the pioneering curator, H.F.E. Peake, who lived at Boxford and was responsible for making Newbury Museum one of the best in the country.

Up beyond the oak stairs and panelled walls – a treat in themselves – we find what made Newbury important in the first place. Leaving aside the table ware of the Middle Ages, records of crime and punishment and a stuffed Peregrine – a disguised security guard? – we reach the Cloth Industry: account books, indentures and apprentices' certificates, a woollen burial pall with the Weavers' Arms woven into it – as lively in colouring today as when it was made more than 200 years ago. It says much for those early dyeing and fulling arts which are here fully described. There are clocks and barometers of the period – and a wash mangle, such as I remember my mother using! But who, I ask, would mangle the coachman's caped coat, so strong and well-constructed to keep out the cold? Or the elegant groom's jacket with its many embossed brass buttons and cardinal red cuffs? Skip the ladies' bonnets, bodices, gloves, dresses and shoes in the next room. On to the Civil War, where television's Jon Snow and son are robustly commenting on a video of the First and Second Battles of Newbury. Prince Rupert's dash, the King's mistakes, the to and fro of fortunes ending in the final denouement up north are all convincingly recounted. Yes, yes, you nod, as if you have actually been there and can confirm the account. But what takes your attention, after the grisly halberds,

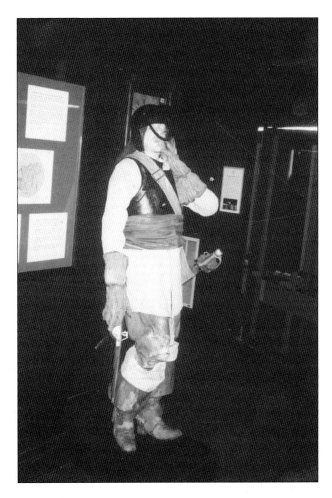

An exhibit of a Civil War soldier.

are the cumbersome, bucket-like helmets. Are they leather? They look like cast-iron! Defying thoughts of gore and gruesomeness, however, is the life-like figure of a soldier in his buff battle dress, vizor, breast plate and long leather gloves and even longer boots. We are warned not to touch him; he is free-standing and vulnerable. He holds his pistol lowered by his side. He has either given up or won. He wears a fetching cummerbund of orange silk. Yes, I think he has won. He is making a victory salute.

You come down to earth in the agricultural section: a cross-cut saw, such as I and my brother used on the farm; pictorial accounts of coopering, coppicing, cultivation and that other kind of weaving, basketry. Finally, you may take a flight of fancy in a balloon. But I shall return again and again in my mind to the orange-cummerbunded warrior and the straight-toothed elephant, untouchably preserved.

CHAPTER NINE

Muscle Up!

'Life isn't all beer and skittles,' says Parson Hughes in *Tom Brown's Schooldays*, 'but beer and skittles or something better of the same sort, must form a good part of every Englishman's education.' He then goes on to describe back-swording and wrestling, 'the most serious holiday pursuits' of the Vale of White Horse. But I have to go to P.H. Ditchfield, another Berkshire parson, to really relish the brute physicality of these tough Downsmen's sports. 'Fifty years ago,' that is about Tom Brown's

Frilsham Common in snow.

time, 'it was the regular custom when two carters stopped at a wayside public-house for the men to shake hands first, in token of friendship, and then indulge in the pastime of cut-legs or kick-shins. The former consisted of the men standing apart and lashing each other's legs with their long whips till one cried "Hold"; while in kick-shins each man took firm grip of his opponent by twisting both hands in the overlapping collar of his smock frock, and then kicking with his hob-nailed boots at the other's shins.' No wonder Tom Brown was 'a robust and combative urchin,' well prepared for Dr Arnold's public school. In the same series – the *Victoria History* – I read about the Berkshire's own public schools, including Wellington College which 'sprang into existence from a subscription from the army, including several Indian regiments . . .' One wonders how many boys, nourished by Hughes's more-than-beer-and-skittles doctrine, went on to run the Empire. Indeed, one must assume that King Alfred himself may have been brought up on earlier, even tougher feats of endurance – the secret perhaps of his strength against the Danes.

These and other 'entertainments' occupied me in a period of enforced inactivity before my 'Spring Offensive' on the Ridgeway.

Now, on 21 March, the vernal equinox, I tell myself to 'muscle up'. I go on my promised Damaskfield walk. It is bright and cold – just what the carters of old enjoyed! I tumble down the field to Hawkridge Wood, past the Kennels – stick in hand, in case needed – and down a lovely wide, inviting track which leads, surprisingly, to someone's front door. There are two cars outside, but no one answers the door, though I ring twice. I cross a small field but meet a barbed-wire fence. I re-investigate, but there are no signs of life apart from children's shoes by a side door and an army of game cockerels who seem to have the run of the place, outnumbering a few less conspicuous hens. Free-range, for them – but 'No Thoroughfare' for me. I retrace my steps to the road and enquire of a lady at a cottage what has happened to the path. 'New people', she says.

The road leads down to the river, anyway. I easily regain the public path. I travel straightforwardly on. The sun tells me I am going west. Until, by some mischance, he lights up my face and I realise I am veering south. I am looking for 'Burntbush Lane (track)' as the map describes it. I am heading for 'Pit (dis)'. Eventually I come to a plantation of what appear to be gorse and laurel saplings sheathed in plastic and a high fence to keep out deer. Brambles strew my way. Cottages suggest I am nearing the road – any road. There is no way out except by a break in the hedge. I realise I am on the Marlston road, that is too far south and west, but near a short cut to Well House which will lead me back to the track to Damaskfield Copse. This turns out to be the most beautiful part of the walk: coppiced hazel, long-tailed tits, clearly-marked paths, larch and birch breaking into leaf, sun-filled fields, coppices – among

The lane near Damaskfield.

Six ways to choose from!

them Damaskfield – mounting to the motorway. A Toyota pick-up is parked by Birch Cottage. 'Nice day,' I say to the man, poised to drive off. I innocently ask where I am. 'I am trying to get to Eling.' 'I'm going there,' he says. 'Jump in.' He is the nicest man I have met all day. Fresh-faced, freckled, smiling into the sun. 'Just move that gun.' It lies just where I am going to put my foot. It is a twelve-bore. 'I'll put it behind me.' 'Are you the keeper?' 'Yes – bin 'ere twenty-six years.' 'I guessed you were from the Gamecock Feeds bags and bins around the place. Heard the hoarse cry of the carrion crow, just now.' 'They're the worst.' he swears – but even the thought of the carrion crow can't take away that look of the boy which certain men never lose. We cross the motorway by an overhead bridge which you would hardly know was there. It would have presented me with doubts. 'It hasn't been here long. We used to drive straight across.' Keepers are sure of their rights of way. 'There's a public path from Eling Farm back to the river?,' I say. 'Yes, I'll drop you right on it.' I tell him about previous walks I've done in this area. He doesn't know the origin of the name Damaskfield, but agrees it is a beautiful, south-facing field which might easily have grown flax in the past. The track from the farm leads down to a most attractive part of the Pang. An ash tree, with its old seed-clusters still hanging like rags about it, still manages to exhibit that feminine grace which characterises most trees in spring; but a full-grown ash striking an attitude, alone in a field by the river, with high, white cumulus clouds overhead and a green slope of pasture rising to young larch woods beyond is a sight to put spring into the step of even an eighty-year-old nearing the end of his journey. Add to that, a man in a blue bobble hat forking a bonfire by the ford. 'There's an owl box in that ash,' I say. 'Yes, and there was an owl in it till the clay pigeon shoot frightened it off.' 'Are there any kingfishers?' 'Not lately.' 'The water's very clear.' 'We used to scoop it up wi' our 'ands an' drink it – we wouldn't do it now, though. Trout used to play around by the banks, an' we'd scoop them up, too!'

Another happy outdoors man, laughing like a boy, the white smoke of his bonfire blown away by the wind to join bobbles of cloud in the sky.

CHAPTER TEN

From One Green Valley to Another

I have been so lucky to have lived in two such beautiful Berkshire villages as Boxford and Frilsham, each with its distinctive green valley and life-giving river. Valleys are like their associated hills: there is always another one beyond. And rivers, perpetually renewing themselves, rejuvenate even the most casual observer. They are extra-dimensional.

When I retired, I bought myself a bike. I bought myself a dog. I was determined not to rot indoors. Our village's dependence on the river, the meadows and the trees was nowhere better illustrated than in the delightful group of dwellings clustered round the church. A pair of crucks at either end, fashioned from the whole trunks or branches of oak naturally curved to meet

Our cottage at Boxford.

Sheep on Boxford Common.

at the top, supported the rest of the framing; lath of split hazel was used with mud from the river puddled with chalk and matted with cow-hair for the wattle and daub infilling; reed from the river was at hand for the thatch. I was beginning to SEE! Soon, I learnt from the experience of having our sixteenth-century cottage rethatched that the uncovering of a roof reveals small skeletons, wasps' nests and old newspapers as well as prompting speculation about the history of the house and its previous inhabitants.

If you live in an old house, you believe in ghosts. You have to. Boxford's houses are full of ghosts. They are fairly harmless, being mostly of the 'footstep' or 'smell' variety. The one at White Cottage is supposed to be only a footstep ghost, but I know better. He is smelly as well. A cloud, vinegary and damp, descends on you and settles in your living room, especially on cold and cheerless days. He comes to keep you company. He smells like those old hessian sacks that farm workers used to wear over their shoulders to keep off the rain. He is there, ever and anon, though you are not.

Oliver's Cottage, just by the church, is said to have a ghost that is a real exhibitionist. On a certain night in November, however tightly gates, doors and windows of the cottage may be shut, in the morning they will all stand open. What a performance! And what a stage for the little charmer to perform on!

Boxford church in snow.

You cannot push Boxford into the past tense. Despite its great age, it exists with its river and its ghosts in a sort of timeless present – almost outside time itself it takes its name from the berroc or box tree which once grew thickly on the slopes of Hoar Hill. The same word is thought to have given rise to the county's ancient name of Berrochescire – though James Edmund Vincent contends that it came from the Saxon name for the bear which once roamed in places like Bear Wood.

Whatever the truth, it is certain that nothing was written down until the appearance of Ricardus, a monk of whom we know little but who has endeared himself to me.

'Go to Boxora,' said the abbot, 'and christianise the people there.' (This I read in Elsie Huntley's *Boxford Barleycorn*.) The year was 1190 AD, and the abbot, the Abbot of Abingdon. Berrochescire has been Latinised. Time has been telescoped again. I am aboard a boat on the river, slily observing Ricardus who needs all his spiritual and physical powers to carry out his commission. As well as the souls of these peasants of Boxora, he has charge of 30 acres of land by the river, for which he has paid five shillings in rent. He is required to plough an acre of this specially for his lord the abbot, sow it with his own seed, provide his lord with hay and corn – the best, of course – and render an account of everything to the Lord Abbot of Abingdon under whose rule this place, like most of Berrochescire, is held. I see Ricardus as popular and strong, making light of his many tasks, going gaily to work, cheered by the nightingale's song in spring, loving nature and God – though not perhaps the abbot – and believing himself always by service set free.

To me, however, the most 'alive' former resident of Boxford is Oliver Sansom; but he is also the most elusive. He died in 1710 – but not before he had written a marvellous, but totally humourless, journal: *The Life of Oliver Sansom, Shewing his Convincement of the Truth, and the Exercises, Tryals and Sufferings which came upon him for his Obedience Thereunto* (etc.)

A Quaker, he was so little concerned about matters corporeal, and so totally committed to the principle of the inner light that he left us no inkling of his outward appearance, even when young. I picture him as small and gingery – a somewhat nimble but testy gnome in a straw hat, liable to go off pop.

Classically educated, he was constantly exercising his mind, weighing and considering – and keeping the score! Even more important, he was constantly exercising his soul: to the frequent discomfort and dismay of the only other people of Boxford who considered themselves educated; the lawyers and the priest. Oliver's war with the latter, the Revd James Anderton, M.A., was a multi-round contest fought over nine years between a heavyweight bruiser, supported by nearly all in authority at the time, and the little Quaker left-hander who literally claimed he had light on his side.

There were a few pre-match confrontations – not surprising in the circumstances. Oliver owned the small farm next to the church; and the rector, whom Oliver always called the priest, lived opposite – so close, in fact, that whenever Oliver was hosting a Friends' meeting and James was playing cards with his friends, the latter was able to see and hear what was going on across the road.

'Quakering again?' he would say the next day as if he thought his opponent had stolen a march on him in training. Thus, by the preliminary, time-honoured taunts and verbal lunges – mostly on the part of the incumbent – the contest was set up.

Caught in the middle, as it were, between two sparring cockerels was Oliver's devoted little pullet of a wife. Jane continued for a time to be faithful to the church of her upbringing – and Oliver's – until, as he records, 'the Lord was pleased to hear my prayers on her behalf.' Then, 'the Priest went after rough and forcible ways to have me driven from the truth.'

Sir Thomas Dolman, JP, of Newbury, no less, became the referee. He sent Oliver a warrant to appear at the Petty Sessions at Speenhamland to swear on oath of allegiance. Oliver would not swear. Neither would he doff his hat.

Fisherman's seat by the Lambourn.

After another fierce round with Anderton he decided to withhold his tithe. Oliver was served with a warrant of distraint. The Tything Man, Church Wardens and the Overseer of the Poor (the Boxford Boxing Board of Control) all met at Oliver's house and with scales weighed out twelve bales of hay. A new warrant was issued and he was brought forcibly to the Sessions. Oliver would not swear. Fines followed – and deprivations. The Tytheman took his winnowing fan. Oliver still refused to pay.

Oliver and his Friends were summoned to the Three Swans Inn at Hungerford. They were all convicted, mainly by false evidence and Oliver was dumped in jail at Reading for 3 months. (Strangely, he had dreamed of this three days before.) And what seems even worse to our twenty-first century minds is that Oliver's manservant with the marvellously apposite name of Cowless was thrown into jail at Abingdon. Jane must have felt like Elijah: 'I, even I, only am left . . .'

A proud patriarch on the Lambourn.

It was at this point that Oliver acted with the greatest nobility. After lying sick (the beginnings of his smallpox?) for a fortnight, his worries mounting, he obtained leave of his keeper to walk home – 18 or 20 miles. Ill and crestfallen, he was forced to hide, not daring to be seen. But he was at home, and with his wife. Finally, recovering a little, he returned to jail to serve out his term.

Released, he continued his meetings. The Justices continued to throw him into jail. His longest sentence was 3 years. Bailiffs, on orders from the rector, took away his horses and impounded his cows, leaving them 8 days without food. Jane was desperate. Friends stood surety and the cows were released. But the officers of the law continued to harry her, even taking loads of hay from her field. The little brown hen must have felt down, but she continued to get up and dust herself off. And the little cock Quaker bounced back.

The priest then set up a terrible cry. 'I will root Oliver out of the town,' he crowed. He would have him publicly burned. As it was, no one would do business with Oliver. The miller was told not to grind his corn. Cowless, threatened with jail again, left in 1667. Finally, the church tower fell down, right by Oliver's door.

It was a terrible, unremitting conflict, fought out in our small village against a background of national disasters: plague, famine and fire.

The sympathy of the villagers was now more with Oliver. When he was put in a cage to be pelted by Fair Day crowds in Newbury Market Square, the constable could not find the key. Set in the stocks, the officer omitted to fasten him in and Oliver slipped away – only to find that Anderton had sold his horse for £4 5s. which Oliver said was worth £6. He was elusive, our Oliver, as I have said – and he kept the score. You could not pin him down.

It would be tedious to recount all his feinting and weaving, his smart left jabs to James Anderton's rather pendulous jowl. We know that he (Anderton) drank and ate too much – and, rather sadly, died of a black discharge.

As for Oliver, he skipped away to Abingdon. Charity Anderton, the priest's widow and her son continued to hound him while he remained in Boxford. Abingdon, however was a great centre for Friends. Oliver traded in linen, serge and books; but moths ruined his cloth and quantities of books were lost. He was always in debt and suffered more warrants of distraint.

But so buoyant was he that he even sailed to Ireland – being happily becalmed off the coast of Liverpool – and travelled to England, even to darkest Shrewsbury, shedding the inward light. He died in 1710, almost, it seems, the moment he set down his pen after composing his account of the 'many remarkable passages' in his life. He was eight years older than Bunyan and only eighteen years younger than Milton. Humourless as his prose shows him to have been, he was, I think, as sweet as a nut from one of his own hazel trees. It seems impossible, when you look round his lovely little thatched dwelling, his riverside orchard and fields, the barns, the saddlery, the ancient rope-walk where honeysuckle scents the air, that this was a veritable cockpit for him and his little saintly wife, Dame Pertelote. But I have a feeling that they revel in the dust.

*   *   *

Just down the road from Oliver's Cottage stands the mill. It was one of at least two mills in Boxford – and one of perhaps two dozen in the Lambourn Valley when millers held a position in society and aggrandised themselves at the expense of their hard-pressed customers, the farmers. Now they are elegant, inert, silent, asleep. I start out early, leaving the houses of the valley and the mossy roadside barns slumbering in my wake. Walking I love, but even more I love to run. Stable companion to Pheidippides, I would like to have been.

I am startled by sheep – all sorts of sheep, down by the river on my right. Jacobs and Herdwicks, old Dorset horned – a motley tribe. Some look like

Boxford Mill.

goats – are goats! A sanctuary, perhaps? For donkeys also, ponies, geese, and swans . . . all in a happy confraternity down by the water's edge.

I pass East Garston, cradled in the valley on my right, and come panting to Eastbury. Panting, not with tiredness, but with excitement. Here, in the church, is the window engraved by Lawrence Whistler to the memory of Edward and Helen Thomas who lived at Spring Cottage. I think of Lob, 'whose sheep grew fat and he himself was merry. . . . One of the lords of No Man's Land, good Lob who is not dead, till millers cease to grind men's bones for bread.' I pass Rose Cottage which my step-son Jonathan rescued from dereliction and rebuilt in the 1970s. He first encountered his neighbour, Mrs Heard, when she was rebuilding her chimney – and she was in her eighties.

✳   ✳   ✳

'Come unto me all ye that are weary and heavy laden and I will give you rest.' That is the welcome you see written over the lychgate of Lambourn church; and at the door of the church I meet Bill, who warmly invites me to climb to the top of the tower.

Lambourn church.

Bill is a man in a million, one of Michael's angels, a servant of the Lord. He is small, with a gentle stoop that suits his natural courtesy; his kindly eyes are brown as acorns or real ale. He is ready to oblige.

'I'll show you the picture of my father and his choir of fifty-two,' he says. To the vestry, stick in hand, he goes parting the curtain and beckoning me, as to an inner temple where the portrait is proudly displayed. He leads me across the transept to the organ, to one side of which is a door, to which he takes a key. We trundle round to the back. The organ, magnificent in front, is stoutly enclosed at the sides by rectangular boxwork palisades; at the back it is like a ship's hold. Somewhere on the way, he points to the place where the handle used to be – the bellows handle which he used to pump. Pride swims in his eyes.

A little way along the nave, he shows me the old doorway to the tower, blocked up as a result of a row between the ringers and the vicar.

'I don't know,' he says, with a deprecating smile and a shake of his head. the cloud soon passes however as he shows me the window dedicated to Charles James Mabberly, organist here for forty-one years, died 10th October 1935.

'My dad,' he says. 'And now we'll go and wind the clock.'

Outside we have to go because of those squabbling bell-ringers and their vicar years gone by. He finds another key, another door, and up we go, by nineteen steps, by twenty-seven, by another seven, I think – and then lose count. Up to the bell chamber, which is astonishingly roomy, airy, light and warm. Up next to the clock; and only then do I understand why Bill likes coming here. It, too, is strangely cased about. Is another key produced? I cannot tell. Bill's movements are so deft. While I am marvelling at the superstructure he has unfolded the doors.

'See that pin? Pull it out.' I had better do as I am told. By much fumbling and repetition of Bill's instructions, I manipulate the key. Did I say key? It is more like the starting handle of an old Alvis.

'About sixty today – I was late winding him last night.'

I wind and count – but soon lose count, partly because of excitement, partly because of what Bill is doing on the other side.

'Do you have to wind the one on the left as well?' Fatuous question! There are two dials.

'Thank you for helping me wind my clock,' Bill says, when we have put all to rights. It is his clock, you see, this maze of cogs, shuttles and fly-wheel which Bill calls the Governor.

'Simple', he says, giving the latter an airy spin. 'Now you'd like to see the view.' The tower, I have read, is twelve hundred feet, so if the steps we now take number only a half of that . . . ? I keep thinking of Bill's age, his arthritis and his hernia.

The view from the top of the tower.

He allows me, as always, to go first. By ladder, and with the help of a hand-rope, we complete the first stage. Then we spy the view. There is a little window, a slit, at the base of the turret, which is reassuring; we know we are still on earth. Then comes the final ascent, by tiny clockwise steps worn by pilgrims of past ages to the top. We emerge by a tiny gnome's door onto the roof. Did I say roof? It is like a courtyard; the tower is like a small castle's keep; each cloud-capped pinnacle, a small landowner's folly. We pussyfoot about on lead, sensing the silence of the spheres. We gaze over the parapet, each crenellation of which is shoulder-high to Bill. They seem surprisingly firm, these airy choppings-out of stone. I even lean on one.

'You can see the motorway some days,' says Bill. He points out the Universal Stores, Oxford Street, Newbury Street, the library, where his father's house once was – where Bill was born.

'And there's my car.' You could knock me down with a feather. I supposed he lived quite near the church.

'No, there's where I live!' He points to a line of white houses on the edge of the town. They don't call it a town, but it is. I risk a photograph, a little unsteadily. Then we take a last look over the valley – Bill's valley, old Ricardus's valley – my valley now.

'I worked on the little railway for twenty-seven years, rising to be a signalman,' he says. We can just see the tree-lined track.

I do not ask him how many years he has wound the clock. 'God's timekeeper', I christen him in my mind. We trundle down, and I still fail to count the steps. Bill would know; but I suspect he is as indifferent to numbers of steps, as he is to numbers of years.

'That's it, then, for another twenty-four hours.' He locks the bottom door. 'Coming down is worse than going up.' He has had one knee operation and is waiting for another. He'll have his hernia done, when there's a bed.

CHAPTER ELEVEN

Looping the Loop

*'One of the pleasantest things in the world is going
a journey; but I like to go by myself.'*

Well said, Hazlitt. If I had a pocket Hazlitt, I would take him with me everywhere. He is much more fun than Richard Jefferies, Edward Thomas or H.J. Massingham. I first came across Hazlitt as a raw youth at grammar school and have loved him ever since. 'No young man believes he shall ever die.' What an arresting thought that is! Then he rounds off his essay on *The Feeling Of Immortality in Youth* with something approaching consolation for growing old: 'The only true retirement is that of the heart; the only true leisure is the repose of the passions.'

On a down looking north: Uffington White Horse.

In the third week of Lent, I am in need of consolation. The anticyclone is holding; up there on the Ridgeway all the kingdoms of the world are spread out in a moment of time; and I am forced to stay at home. It gives me, however, an opportunity for reflection – which Hazlitt, no doubt also savoured with plentiful cups of thick, black tea.

I came to know the Ridgeway in 1970. On 10 August, my step-son Jonathan – seventeen, sunny and fearless – set off from Yattendon on his Welsh cob, Inca, to ride to Shropshire where we were going to live. He reported that night that he had pitched camp and tethered the horse in a field at Compton Beauchamp – a stone's throw from Wayland's Smithy, if he, or rather the horse, had need of a shoe!

It was with a similar trust in serendipity that I set out in March 1990 to walk from our front door in Boxford, where we were living then, over the same Downs, Cotswolds, Malverns, South Shropshire and Welsh border hills. I drew a bee-line map of the more or less direct north-westerly route, bought a pair of boots, dusted off an old haversack and hoped for the best. I was not yet seventy then. This time, I face a shorter, more familiar task with, as Hazlitt would have it, less passion but a good deal more serenity.

Sitting at home, I ponder the possibility that some landscapes, like some people, have more personality than others. 'Life is a pure flame, and we live by an invisible sun within us,' said Sir Thomas Browne. (This, one of Hazlitt's many glinting quotations, which light up his thoughts.) Certainly the Ridgeway has character more than most. It is 3,000 years old; high, wide and handsome; stretches for 30 or more miles in either direction; and carries the traveller, says Edward Thomas, as if along the battlements of a castle. It takes you up and sweeps you along, swinging its arms and offering you boundless, variegated views, sprinkled with cloud shadows and far-flung hangers of trees. You ride, as it were, on the giant's shoulders, your head in the sky. Coombe Hill and all those other Berkshire ridges have been like prep-school runs compared to this international steeplechase!

Trouble is, I'm not going on a straight run; I'm looping the loop, orbiting Berkshire, facing stiff fences, the occasional Canal Turn and, now and then, a water jump. Trouble is, also, I may not stick to or stay the course. I may be seduced by Applepie Hill or the tithe barn at Great Coxwell – or by some other attraction which our meddlesome planners have declared out of bounds. The Ridgeway – like those old barns at Aldworth – is a steady-state universe, co-existing with the Big Bang, expanding universe of Didcot, Swindon, Oxford and Reading. Even on its lofty, clearly defined path, you cannot escape the effects of modern life: tractors and muck-spreaders and, of course, 4x4s. But you can hope for a fine, clear day and a snatch of a solitary skylark's song.

CHAPTER TWELVE

Ariel and Skylarks: Riding on Air

'That's my dainty Ariel,' I say, squeezing him into the back of the car like a racehorse into the stalls. I tacitly apologise for the indignity; the space is tight, and his head is forced back to allow the boot to come down; but soon we will both be set free.

First, we head for East Ilsley, The Firs, Stanmore Road; then, from our starting point above the village, we silently swoop down to West Ilsley where we call at the stables to see Steppe Dancer and his lad, Gerry, who is just mucking him out and laying out a fresh bed. 'He won at Kempton on Saturday,' he says, laconically, forking the straw round his feet. 'And Tromp, next door'. That's what I like to hear: a small stable with two winners in one day. Dennis, the trainer, comes back from riding out with the first string. He promises me a picture of Steppe Dancer – if I remind him. I feel I have won a race myself.

Next, we trundle down the long, grass-verged, drive to beautiful Hodcott, surrounded with green lawns and wide-awake daffodils. This is a private world, quietly coming to life through the fog: a saddle deposited here, a whip and a bridle there. Small, helmeted figures move about on silent feet as if in a prelude to a ballet; horses' heads nod over box-doors, framed by grilles either side. Jocks bustle about –lasses and lads – grooming their charges for the performance of the day. These are the two-year-old colts, whose silky coats are just beginning to shine under dandy brush and curry comb. And under those coats – some already rugged and saddled – there are the tendons, sinews and muscles, not to mention the blood, of the thoroughbred racehorse, quivering with excitement and power. You see it in their fully-confident, large, liquid eyes. And the smiles on the faces of their proud handlers. The controlled silence is part of the show. It is a ballet without music; an oft-repeated mime; almost a shadow-play. Then, just as the fog disperses and the light comes in, there is a drum-tap of hooves; one misty grey colt and his rider advance from the back of the stage, followed by bays and chestnuts stepping airily onto the scene, all cloaked in the black and red colours with the monogram MC. The riders, moving in unison with their mounts, display an almost reckless nonchalance. Gradually, the rest of the corps-de-ballet peel off downstage and

East Ilsley High Street.

The view from the churchyard.

join the growing throng. One or two show signs of breaking ranks. One silky show-off is airborne, attempting a solo rodeo, but is soon brought into line. The jocks are all legged-up in turn by the attentive head lad who steadies their departure. It is an equine *Daphnis and Chloe* rehearsal, traditionally choreographed and exquisitely performed which I am privileged to attend; and every one of these potential racing stars is a winner this morning. A dream come true.

*   *   *

Bury Down Lane is clamped in a cold, grey mist as we head on up to the Ridgeway. A pale, pewter disc, more like the face of the moon than the sun, peeps through the blanket of cloud and goes back to bed. Daffodils, like torches, light the gateway to a farm – the last lamps of civilisation, for a while. Everything is blotted out; trees blurred; horizons obliterated. This is no-man's-land. Signs to the Ridgeway point east; point west. You must choose your course now – live or die. The first landmark, west, is the monument to Robert

Boyd Lindsay, Baron Wantage of Lockinge. It records his valour at the battles of Inkermann and Alma, 1854, in the Crimean War. Several years ago, I sat on its stone pediment and lunched in sunshine with two young friends; today, the stone is cold to the seat and partly grassed or mossed over; the inscriptions are worn, almost to illegibility and there is some defacement by graffiti. I stumble away, regretting the dishonour done and the 'transitoriness of this mortal life.' Even the banana in my hand is tasteless and frozen – the peel a black embarrassment. Suddenly, however, a snatch of a skylark's song restores my spirits. I bowl along on Ariel on turf that has been bowled along for thousands of years. There is no stopping us now. Even the skylarks, perched along the wires which fence off the track, are amazed. They spark into life again, swing away, soar and sing. Ariel and I do the same – without actually gaining lift-off. But here, on top of the world, you are never totally earthbound. You are close

The monument to Baron Wantage.

On the White Horse.

to the moonwalker's weightlessness and freedom from earthly concerns. Scutchamer's Knob! A mark on the map as memorable as the Sea of Tranquillity. Lapwings cry: 'Peewit, Peewit!' Then, in a clearing of cloud, their green-black coats flash in the sun. Theirs is the craziest dip-dip-and-swing, swooping and soaring aerobatic display to be seen. It used to be common, but now is rare.

For old time's sake, I dip down to Letcombe Regis, to visit the pub. The Sparrow, where I quaffed and laughed with those young friends several years ago, has gone; but I find fish and chips at The Greyhound – and the unwelcome voices of Paisley and Adams on the television. I escape to the quiet of the graveyard. The rather dark, thatched Old House, opposite the church, had been sold – for what astronomical sum, I wonder – but the church itself towers above its daffodils on a green eminence in full sun – an exhilarating reminder that life goes on after death. I retrace my steps, uphill past the stud farm – pregnant with life. Willows, too. Court Hill YHA. (Not open till the weekend.) Back to the life-enhancing turf of the Ridgeway. Back by long, erratic, bone-shaking, bike-rattling down-hill gallops to East Ilsley and my patient, much-looked-down-upon car.

Letcombe Regis church.

To the North-West Frontier

The next day, we are off again. 'That's my dainty Ariel. Trust me, I'm your Prospero.' We are going to Lambourn – as famous for its racehorses as Newmarket, they say. But more relaxed. That is the opinion of Peter Walwyn, who should know. I meet him at Windsor House. He is retired now, but still as active in the racing world as ever – if not more so. He takes me by car on a tour of his domain – his and twenty or thirty other trainers who operate on the expansive downs around the town. How big this area is, no one who visits Lambourn village for its wonderful church and busy shops, can possibly imagine. The acreage of sweeping downland, grazed and trodden by sheep and horses to their mutual advantage, is vast. Beyond Upper Lambourn and stretching into Oxfordshire, the hills are scattered with sarsen stones left behind by an ancient glacier, similar to those that characterise the Marlborough Downs; but just around Lambourn itself the trainers nurse and groom the turf as carefully as the horses they train on it. It is daily inspected, rolled and harrowed and brought into condition. It is made of the best fescues, fresh-green, firm yet springy and soft. It is the product of centuries of care.

An unlikely winner at Newbury Races.

And Peter Walwyn will tell you how much work and money has gone into it –
and how much more remains to be done.

'We haven't done yet,' says Peter when we return to Windsor house, after he
has toured the polytracks, talked to fellow trainers, watched strings of horses
going out and strings coming in, pointed out new areas of development,
chatted to someone trying to coax her horse to walk in the river, viewed the
swimming pool, the village centre – its memorials to racing and generous
leisure equipment, the old stables ear-marked for retired or disabled staff, the
houses for the present staff named after famous horses of the past and praised
the efforts of the whole community to secure the future. He is like a beacon,
luminous with hope; but not just hope – rather the energy that produces such
light. Modesty prevents him saying so, but it is clear that he has done more for
the community of Lambourn, its 3,000 people and 2,000 horses, than anyone
else.

While he goes indoors for a moment, I link up with Christina, wife of Harry
Dunlop who now runs the yard. She keeps Berkshire pigs; and one of her sows

Christina and her pedigree
Berkshire pigs.

is a champion. I, having resisted temptation all morning, am fairly itching for a photograph. Proud Christina and her Truffle – what else would you call this dainty eater? – are quickly snapped up. Then, back in the house, Peter shows me his paintings: those on the wall, old and relevant to his illustrious heritage, but also his own, unframed water colours. This man, so steeped in history and careful of tradition, does not sit back or stand still. He is moving on. His sense of colour is highly developed – whose in racing wouldn't be? His skill with the brush is remarkable. And he has written a book, a copy of which he signs for me. My Lord, what a morning!

The afternoon looks like being dull as I pedal into Oxfordshire. The only thing that enlivens Weathercock Hill are the sheep – mostly white ewes with totally black lambs – and the peewits which have found a field with what appears to be the remains of an old maize crop, undisturbed at the moment – possibly even forgotten about. Their joy at finding it matches my joy at seeing them. Winged scallywags, like the equally hardy and wily skylarks, it is perhaps better for them to nest here, I think, than on the adjoining barley or wheat which is constantly sprayed – or the rape which would choke and smother them altogether. This track is so completely removed from human habitation, I can see not a house in any direction. I hear what seems at first to be traffic on a road below, but it turns out to be only a tractor bumbling about in its own halo of dust in the distance. There is just the hint of a village in the mist – but so far off it might be somewhere in the foothills of Tibet. Either side of the main track run minor public footpaths, marked simply PF, but I dare not follow them. I stick to my belief that while I have the sun at my back I will eventually reach the Ridgeway. A quick look at the map tells me I have come over Fognam Down and am possibly heading for Wayland's Smithy; but it is not till I meet a young lady with a dog – the first sign of life on earth this afternoon – that I am assured I am right. And yes, there, at the bottom of a slope, is the familiar tree- and-scrub-lined path to my goal. Here are no soft pussy willows: only stark blackthorn and elder – and, surprisingly, a colony of grand beech trees which surround the tomb. It is described as an ancient monument; possibly over 5,000 years old. But it has a strange immediacy. The sun filters through the beech boughs, softening the stones and casting lively shadows on well-trodden paths between areas of grass. It is so finely sculpted by weather and time that it is an irresistible subject for a charcoal sketch. Its moods are too evanescent for a painting – or even for a photograph. Here, you feel, you must dwell. Abandon all thought of time. We are in another geological time zone where, according to legend, the god-smith Wayland will bide his time not ours; but the waiting will be rewarded.

✳   ✳   ✳

Wayland's Smithy.

'So rough was it in Great Coxwell tithe barn that most of the National Trust's pamphlets (50p) were freely distributed by the wind.' That was in March 1992, when I set out to walk from my front door in Boxford, Berkshire, to my childhood home in the village of Little Ness, Shropshire. I have always loved small, tucked-away places: Daglingworth and the Duntisbournes in Gloucestershire, Dittisham and Tuckenhay in Devon, Hoarwithy and almost all its neighbours in Herefordshire – quietly whisper it – Clunbury, Clunton and Clun. They are mostly bypassed by main roads, which helps to preserve their privacy; and, like personal treasures kept locked away in your own home, you would not dream of disclosing them to nosy-parkers or strangers. Indeed, on that blustery blackthorn-winter day in 1992, I came upon Great Coxwell and its superb barn quite unexpectedly. It compares in my memory with the Golden Gate Bridge and the Palace of Versailles. Can it really have been designed and made by simple Cistercian monks or is it also the product of some supernatural force? *Laborare est orare*!

The interior of Great Coxwell Tithe Barn.

Great Coxwell Tithe Barn.

The internal dimensions are plainly set out in the leaflet: 144 x 38ft, and a floor area of 5,502 sq ft. The enormous double doors stand open at either end, welcoming you in from the wind. Light pours in from open slit windows and the regularly spaced square putlog holes through which the masons' scaffolding passed in construction – and kept the grain aired inside. The roof is a thousand rafters, laths, crucks, trusses and struts, all regularly mounted to support purlins and tiles, the whole supported by twelve oak pillars mounted on stone plinths on either side of the main aisle. It is no surprise that William Morris declared it to be 'unapproachable in dignity, as beautiful as a cathedral, yet with no ostentation of the builder's art . . . the finest piece of architecture in England.'

We will now slip quietly back from this piece of trespassing into Oxfordshire – too magnetic to be resisted – and return via the no-man's-land area which is neither Berkshire, Oxfordshire or Wiltshire watched over by the Royal College of Military Science at Watchfield. Leave the paltry paddocks round Bourton and Bishopstone and head back to the expansive, prairie-like downs above Lambourn where horses and sheep together outnumber men. On reflection, perhaps it is because there is a similar absence of men in the wide open spaces of that tithe barn at Great Coxwell that I feel it still belongs to Berkshire by right.

Weathercock Hill.

No doubting, however, to whom the Lambourn Valley belongs: it belongs to me! From Ashdown Park it is all downhill; past the little black lambs on Weathercock Hill, past the veterinary centre, past the stable entrances with their distinctive white clock-towers and weather vanes, past the parish church – the Cathedral of the Downs, whose clock is stopped at ten past ten! – to Lower Bockhampton, where I know of another barn – but we can't call there now. We are hurrying home through Eastbury, East Garston and Great Shefford, where the sun catches the round tower of the church, like an eighteenth-century stone marmalade pot. A little way downstream lies one of the most tucked-away treasures of Berkshire. You have to cross the river by a farm, ask for the key and pray, as you prayed at Great Coxwell, that you may have the place to yourself. Here, where the King of Mercia once had his palace, is the little redundant church of East (or Little) Shefford. The Fettiplaces once owned all this land, and here you will find their tomb. Here, in this secret place, where it is such a pleasure to be alive, it must be a great privilege to be dead.

Someone once wrote: 'The Tracys, the Lacys and the Fettiplaces own all the manors, the parks and the chases.' They date back to before the big barn at Great Coxwell, but the last of this great family passed away in 1805: cause of death, apoplexy – in a Burford pub. The family had once owned land in fifteen counties, but, according to Mr Vincent, Childrey and Little Shefford in Berkshire, and Swinbrook (where Evelyn Waugh came from) in Oxfordshire, were their principal seats.

Inside the church are fragments of wall paintings which are said to be among the oldest in the country; but away to one side is the damaged fifteenth-century alabaster tomb of Sir Thomas Fettiplace and his Portuguese wife, Beatrice – damaged, but all the more poignant for being so. One feels, as one does faced by the grand emptiness of Great Coxwell, only gratitude to the preservers of these monuments of the past, whatever their scale, whatever their cost.

Meanwhile the little clear chalk stream, the Lambourn, runs on. It breaks into multiple channels, spreads over fields and creates jungly backwaters, green islands and blue, transparent pools. It is girlish and delightful as it skips along, the wind loosening, as it were, the braids of its hair. It is as limpid and lovely as the Test. There is a period – the first fortnight in May – when any fool can catch a trout in this valley. But, being only about 15 miles long and by nature secretive, it is little known – except to coots and connoisseurs. Moorhens step across green rafts of water crowfoot without getting their feet wet. The river, road and railway track – that of the old Lambourn Light Railway which used to allow the sheep preference in crossing it – run for much of the time in parallel. Here at East Shefford by a bend in the river, trees on

Clear chalk stream, the Lambourn.

either side of the road are haunted by rooks; there is an island with geese, ducks and swans; a heron dips doubtfully down, then swings away. Set back, but surely the most splendidly sited house in the valley, the Mill, is as if floodlit with daffodils, which of all flowers best extend the evening light. But the river says: 'Hurry on down – we'll join the Kennet at Thatcham. Then bowl along the tow-path to Reading – or Hungerford. Whichever way the wind blows.'

Light and Shade: Work and Play

If cycling along the Ridgeway is like riding on air, pedalling along the tow-path is almost like floating on water. It is so level and well-maintained. It is part of the National Cycle Network. It is certainly the most rewarding route into Reading. The whole carnival of life is here. The road, railway, river and canal run side by side. The route is marked by many locks – always with the potential for a unexpected sideshow. Fishermen crouch inconspicuously by the bank, or flaunt their professionalism under coloured umbrellas with trolleys of equipment drawn alongside them; the roofs of houseboats display small gardens

Hannah the boat-horse, resting near Kintbury.

Idyll at Sulhamstead.

of flowers; swans peck at their windows to see if the occupants are ready to share their breakfast yet; coots yelp, moorhens trill; a boy swings from a tree overhanging the water to impress his young female companion – you thought the age of childhood chivalry was dead? The fun starts at the Rowbarge at Midgham where the road bridge has to be lifted and the traffic is held up. Such is the dramatic pace of life hereabouts. Everything slows down by the canal. This is the marvellous aqueous world of alders and willows, reflected white swing bridges, boats with names like Marquis, Tulip and Cat's Whiskers – not to mention Ratty and Mole (Wind In The Willows) and Toad's Escape. There is every kind of bridge, under or over, steel or wood; as there is every kind of gate and gate-fastening on the cyclist's track. Andrew of Cwmbran affords the easiest passage with his silent, self-closing miracles of wood. I struggle with the heavy, tubular steel type that clank and bang and snap at your hand like a dog. Aldermaston has, I think, the finest lock; and the stretch between Tyle Mill and Sheffield Bottom, just above Sulhamstead, is the most idyllic.

Suddenly, however, the whole landscape and waterscape breaks into gravel pits and mountains of stone. Burghfield I try to blot from my mind. Water-skiing and wakeboarding next announce themselves; Reading motor services and Marks & Spencer are only half a mile off. I backtrack and take an alternative route across a field – the longest, most puzzling cross-country run of my life; but it leads back to the designated track, the tow-path, the Cunning Man country restaurant, a police diver recovering what appears to be an iron-age bicycle pump from the bed of the canal, the first wild cherry blossom and my first sight of the concrete towers of modern Reading rake the sky. Gone now are the yellow celandines, dandelion and coltsfoot; the distinctive dark-blue periwinkle and ground ivy; and the bright-eyed speedwell and daisies that have entertained me for the past two hours. Gone, too, the curious, 'hobby-farmed' horned sheep – Dorset-cross? – with their sad, round, owl-like faces; the scarpering, naughty-boy jays, the brilliant, enamel mallards, honking Canada geese and cross-sounding coots – although, surprisingly the usually furtive heron, the cunning man of the bird world, has, it seems, begun to adapt to this slick urban kind of life. Suddenly the sun lights up the House of Fraser and The Oracle; but the National Cycle Network still leads me safely to Blake's Lock Museum, just above the Kennet's confluence with the Thames. Mission accomplished, I can now head up to the Abbey and refresh my memory of Duke Street, Jackson's Corner, the Town Hall and St Lawrence's Church. Gone are the days when I could park my MG just across the river in Sidmouth Street; when I bought my checked cap at Jackson's, which has not worn out in fifty years; sang in the *Messiah* with the Choral Society under Ewart Masser, Eric Few playing the Town Hall organ; and happily drove boys from Earley across Reading to play football against Caversham or Calcot primary schools.

Reading Abbey ruins.

Huntley and Palmer's biscuit factory was one of Reading's focal points then. The A329 was the principal road in and out of the town, known as the Reading Road (west) or the Wokingham Road (east). Earley, where I started teaching, was mostly green fields. It is now one of the biggest conurbations in Europe. No wonder I cling to my memories of the great Victorian Town Hall, St Lawrence's Church and precious remains of the twelfth-century Abbey Church.

The moment you enter the Forbury you enter an alternative world; and the moment you enter the Abbey itself you enter an alternative universe. It is that different in both time and space. The Kennet and Avon Canal now seems like a stripling; Huntley and Palmer's as short-lived as the biscuits which they floated down the canal to ensure fewer breakages.

The Forbury Gardens are as welcoming as ever with the Edwardian-type bandstand and imperial black lion crowning the Afghan war memorial. Mute pomp and circumstance! Previous visits to Blake's Lock have suggested that Reading's glory days were built on the canal – now mainly a tourist attraction – and were fuelled by agriculture as much as by industry. Along with faint echoes of the cloth industry, already declining three centuries before, are photographic evidence of huge Corn Stores and notices telling the visitor that coal as well as corn, salt, seed, hay and straw were all dealt with at the wharf. The range of enterprise and ingenuity of the Victorians is demonstrated by such objects as a stove with the imprint Callas Sons and May Ltd., by emblems and lead fire marks of many assurance companies, by two old wooden fire engines from Woolhampton and Sonning and by a Romany van of Reading manufacture from 1900, with bowed roof stands, recently refurbished, gleaming green and gold with amber glass door and shutter knobs. Never, one is tempted to assert, since the Normans had such wealth been generated in England – and particularly Berkshire – by the work of men's hands, the sweat and foresight of their brows. Not only massed labour forces but the sheer physical and mental energy of individuals, geared to the use of prime natural resources, yielded the increase. The Abbey ruins – here a giant pillar, like the blackened molar of some medieval mammoth, there a stout fragment of a wall – are a solid reminder of the prosperity that these conquerors – not the first, nor the last of immigrants to use this waterway – brought to our land.

Henry Beauclerc, a tablet on one wall tells us, built the Abbey to be his burial place and memorial. It housed possibly 100 monks when it was consecrated by Thomas a Becket in 1164 in the presence of his friend – soon to turn enemy – Henry II. Future sovereigns came; Parliament met here. It was the most powerful abbey in the land.till Henry VIII dissolved it and the last abbot was hanged at the gates. Henry built himself a palace here, last used by Charles I. That is how royal and ancient it is – and, to those who can read the history, free.

A sculpture of a robed figure by Dame Elisabeth Frink in the grounds of Reading Abbey.

Leaving Reading, one is struck by its cosmopolitan air on this wonderfully sunny April day. It is one large leisure centre now, exotic and pedestrianised: a global walkabout. Shops and restaurants have names like Old Orleans, Carbuccios, Vue, Bar Mediterranee, Strada and Walamama; but among all these changes I have not forgotten to renew my acquaintance with Henry West whose memorial still stands in St Lawrence's churchyard: In memory of Henry West who lost his life in a whirlwind at the Great Western Railway station, Reading, 24 March 1840. A rail was erected by his fellow workmen, renewed by his brother George in 1862 and again by his niece in 1920. The present wooden structure was placed there by the Corporation in 1971. Such is the power of Reading to surprise; such is its power to sustain and reinvent itself.

✳   ✳   ✳

'Here come the sun and the great Easter getaway' shouts the *Daily Telegraph*, next day, 3 April. Airports prepare to deal with the threat of chaos . . . Staff brace themselves to check passengers' baggage and ward off explosions. I shall forego all that and seek my pleasures at the Lambourn Trainers' Open Day on Good Friday and, later, the tutti men's revels at Hocktide in Hungerford.

'I slip, I slide, I gloom, I glance . . .' Tennyson's marvellous poem, 'The Brook', runs through my head as I drive up the valley – as it has run for seventy years since I first learnt it by heart at Little Ness – past Boxford, past Weston, past Welford, past Shefford, past East Garston, through Eastbury and the Valley of the Racehorse to crown this celebration of Man's Best Friend.

Deano's Beeno on parade at Lambourn Trainers' Open Day.

Dogs, even ferrets, will vie for our attention at the Lambourn Trainers' Open Day but towering over all is the Thoroughbred – the offspring of the Byerley Turk, the Darley and the Godolphin Arabian. It is one of the astonishing facts of nature that the blood of those eighteenth-century stallions still flows in the veins of the thousands of pure-bred racehorses running in the world today. Just as, I suppose, the same water sparkles down these Berkshire valleys: the Ock, the Dun, the Kennet, the Lambourn to be borne by the Thames out to sea and recycled afresh, perpetually.

The river at Lambourn is hard to pin down – as the Pang is at East Ilsley and Compton. It ducks in and out of sight, as if trying to escape from man's interference. And what obstacles man has put in its path! If I were a professor of town planning I would not offer Lambourn as a model. No wonder the river tries to dissociate itself. Beside the church, which occupies pride of place – but does not appear to command much attention otherwise – there is the heavily restored front to the sixteenth-century almshouses which looks like the entrance to a modern Oxford College. You have to look away from the market place along a little road to the west that leads back to the river, to a striking brick and flint farmhouse and an elegant white one on the corner, apparently empty now but which, I am told, belonged to the doctor. These, I suppose, are the relics of a time, not so long ago, when the parson, the doctor and the farmer were the principal figures in the community – nourishing it, healing it and correcting it by natural authority. It is a different social order now.

I slip, I slide, I gloom – but not for long. I am heading for the stables, which are mostly out of town. Upper Lambourn, in fact, is a healthier, wealthier place to be – making its urban foster-parent seem positively down-at-heel. This is The Big Earner today. While the little river slinks away to the south, the tide of Mammon courses to the north. Trade stands beckon on the showground on one side of the hill. The veterinary centre will be open at eleven. There is a demonstration of farriery at the old chapel all morning. These are not the grumpy old blacksmiths that I remember. They are striplings in eye-shields plunging their tongs into gas-fired cinders and punning white-hot metal on tiny anvils with the quick footwork of Tommy Steele. There is no horse in sight. It's cool, I suppose.

The tiny graveyard of the redundant chapel contrasts sadly with the yards where the trainers house their charges in boxes, some labelled: 'This Horse May Bite.' I am a sucker for show animals: pigs, sheep, cattle, poultry – especially those of the fancier breeds. There is such poetry in their names; such humour in their vain, ridiculous looks! But you cannot ridicule a horse. He – and even more certainly she – is so superior to the gawping crowd of humanity invading these normally secluded and lavishly appointed halls of residence. Schooling is over for the day, so who is studying whom? Here in Mike

Lambourn Almshouses.

Blanshard's yard is Miss Bouggy Wouggy a bay, two-year-old out of Polly Golightly; here, in Noel Chance's National Hunt set-up is 'a horse to follow' in the shape of Jardin de Vienne, a five-year-old grey gelding by Highest Honor, out of Vaguely Money (USA). I feel an incipient itch in my palm. At another yard, one is invited to take a half-share in a filly; alternatively you can win a tiny piece of an untried colt in a raffle. It is surreal; like taking a trip to the moon. My bike keeps me down to earth, one hand on the handle bars, the other firmly in my pocket. Only a keen-eyed youth at the entrance to the showground spots that I have not bought a programme, have not displayed my badge. It is a fair cop. Without our contribution to the funds, Miss Bouggy Wouggy and Jardin de Vienne may never win. But do I really want to eat chips, watch ferret racing and bungee jumping or John Francome and Richard Dunwoody schooling horses over fences? I am, however, still sufficiently drawn to the animals – even the pink-eyed ferrets, stubbornly refusing to travel down pipes to no object except to draw money from the crowd. The Vine and Craven hounds – a depleted pack, minus the horses – turn out, accompanied by two sober men in white coats and black bowler hats but the scheduled terrier racing, which might have run out of control, is called off; part of Fuller's brewery dray has not arrived; the ferrets must perform a second time. You pays your money and you takes your choice. . . .

My spirits are restored at Bockhampton where I recover my car, drink tea and engage in conversation with a friend who has been rebuilding his barn for many years and is now approaching Stage Three. I tell him I am rebuilding Berkshire and have still three stages to go. I cannot hang about. He smiles indulgently; the sleek little Lambourn slips through the willows in his garden: 'for men may come and men may go, but I go on for ever.'

Strange Incident on Applepie Hill

The whole of England seems spread out before you when you reach Applepie Hill. It lies between Aldworth and Compton, on a little slip road that runs between Pibworth and Woodrows Farm. There are not many woods – more lank hedgerows, mostly blackthorn and ivy – in these lean farming lower parts of the downs. (Starveall is a name that occurs more than once.) And Applepie Hill is a mere 165 metres, but the contours gather like small cyclones round the Ridgeway to the north. Little grassy tracks tempt you to stop beside the road. Carpets of celandines. An intrepid young rabbit. A hedgehog, curled up defensively, in vain, against the grilled monster that had mown it down. What pretty faces hedgehogs have – even when tidied away in death! But what is this? A stoat perhaps? But why is it so still? Stoats usually streak across a road like shooting stars across the sky. Stretched out. Little seams run the length of its tummy and round the backs of its legs, each ending in a whorl, an embossed helix, nature's perfect shape, the weasel's trademark, pretty as a fingerprint. And just as unrepeatable.

'It's not the tractors that come along these lanes that kill the pheasants, hares, foxes and squirrels,' you find yourself saying 'It's the BMWs and 4x4s I blame for the carnage on our roads.' Usually there are a couple of magpies cleaning up. Not now. But you must try to rescue this little miracle of design from further crushing. You pick up two handy sycamore sticks from the hedge. Close up, hands trembling, you wonder if such a delicate operation is possible. Might you get more than you bargained for? From sooty nose to untipped tail she is no longer than a man's middle finger. Not as wide! Displaying there her little white bodice and underbelly. Pregnant, perhaps? Is it the sharpness of the eyes and teeth that holds you in a trance? She is as evil in her reputation as a bat, an adder, a hawk. . . .

Well, there's no time to hang about. Riveted by the tiny chestnut spitfire, committing to memory the luxuriance of her chestnut flanks, the touch of lamp-black on her throat, the etching round her eyes, her ears, her flinty grin. . . .

You do not have to wonder long, for, suddenly, like a tiny torpedo boat, she rights herself and ripples away. 'Must have been stunned!' you smile with relief, still holding your sticks in the manner of an Englishman faced with a Chinese meal.

Hocktide at Hungerford: Pageantry, Passion, Plantagenet Pride, Protocol, Posies, Pennies and Punch

I try to come to Hungerford afresh, jettisoning all my mental bric-a-brac, pretending I've never been there; never even heard of it; and the best way to see it, it seems to me, this particular April morning, is by the Kennet and Avon towpath. Ahead of me are the delights of Kintbury, Lower Denford and – when I turn into Bridge Street – my first glimpse of Regency and Victorian Hungerford – a town that still owes everything to successive revolutions in communication, by road, railway, canal – and now, of course, information technology. Two worlds – two universes, even – co-exist and benefit each other here. The old does not give place to the new – indeed, with stunning ostentation, it holds its own. Hungerford, as we shall see, has made a virtue – and a fortune – out of being old.

It is Hocktide at Hungerford, traditionally held in the second week after Easter. This year, there is no holding back. Prompt at eight o'clock, the

Hungerford Town Hall.

constable with his steward appears on the balcony of the town hall, blows his
horn, rings his bell and shouts 'Oyez, Oyez!' Normally, I think this is the most
boring sound on earth. Today, however, in the mouth of this white-headed,
top-hatted master, it is electrifying. And, not content with one cry, he does it
again; steps down into the street and does it again, more lustily each time. His
steward beams like an approving prefect at his headmaster. They cross the
street to The Three Swans Inn. There, on the steps, they are joined in
conversation by a ox-like character in green knickerbockers and waistcoat
with gold buttons, white ruffled shirt and, of course, silver-buckled shoes. I am
near enough to hear his broad Buckinghamshire burr – and to learn that he is
a fellow town-crier. Before I can learn more, the constable is at it again –
accompanied, this time, by the Buckinghamshire Ox, dressed all in green,
gold-buttoned coat and tricorn, feathered hat. Two tutti men appear, one with

Hocktide scenes.

a Tommy Cooper fez, the other looking remarkably like Nick Lumley, the actor. They cross back over to the town hall steps where they are presented with their decorated tutti-poles. This is where the 'extras' come on scene: an Orangeman and a bevy of girls dressed in blue with white bonnets and aprons – but, before our attention can be diverted further, we bystanders and commoners of the Town and Borough of Hungerford (and the Liberty of Sandon Fee) are summoned by the Constable to the serious business of the Court. Away goes that horn; away goes that bell. 'Oyez, Oyez!' This, it turns out, is the true purpose of Hocktide: the solemn reading and remembrance of the rules that bind commoners of the Borough, that is Town and Manor of Hungerford (and the Liberty of Sandon Fee – how W.S. Gilbert would have loved this!) and the penalties for breaking them. The elected jury sits round the long green-baize table, solemn oaths are sworn; a sort of civic Holy

Hocktide at Hungerford.

Matrimony – which, in its way, of course, it is. And it has been going on religiously, every year in Hungerford, according to the letter of the law and in the very same manner of expression, since the time of John of Gaunt, son of Edward III, Duke of Lancaster, who owned all these rich riverside lands. Everything goes forward and is confirmed by the Grace of God, in allegiance to the Queen – and not forgetting the Duke of Lancaster. It takes two hours to perform this wonderful piece of theatre; and – apart from the recitation of lists of names of commoners, present and unpresent – the show is mesmeric. If only our shifty central government were as well-ordered, good-humoured, thorough and respectful as this little local forum we might nationally aspire to the vision of England that Shakespeare put into the mouth of John of Gaunt: This royal throne of kings . . . this happy breed of men. . . .

Realising the frailty of our nature, however, we disperse – the jury and court to its lunch laced with Plantagenet punch, the rest of us to a street taken up with the affairs of everyday life. No evidence of the tutti-men stealing kisses or rewarding ladies with a penny or an orange! I bowl on down past the church to Freeman's Marsh and the banks of the beautiful, free-flowing, minding-its-own-business, clear chalk stream, the Dun.

There is much more to Hocktide in Hungerford than I have been able to convey; there is much more to Berkshire, I am sure; but the thought occurs to me, as it has so often on this glorious spring tour of land- and water-byways of the county, that the Pliocene chalk-bed underlying it is a kind of palimpsest on which man has left no coherent message but drawn, rather like the cave artists, wonderful patterns – some royal, some ancient and all free.

EPILOGUE

Nature's Spring Flower Show

One of my favourite books is Cecil Aldin's *Romance of the Road* in which he presents himself as a showman, 'the precursor', he says, 'of Charles B. Cochran and Bertram Mills, who stood outside his booth before the performance commenced, thumping on his drum and declaiming of the wonders within.' The show is set in 1828, the heyday of coaching in England, in particular along the Bath Road, when the clocks of Piccadilly struck eight on Midsummer Eve, 'eight coachmen adjusted themselves on their box seats and gathered up the reins . . . BANG! BANG! BANG! went the lids, and the western mails started slowly away from the Gloucester Coffee Tavern in Piccadilly on their nightly journey across England.'

I am not a showman; neither have I Aldin's artistic powers. I am, as I said at the beginning, only a 'gawper', a raw country lad. (Indeed, I was lucky enough to see a reconstruction of one of those Bath Road runs in, I think, 1978.) The show, however, that I am pleased to present to the reader is the one that Nature in Berkshire annually provides and which, this year, has been superb. Primroses, kingcups, celandines, archangel, cowslips, gorse and dandelions; violets, bluebells, forget-me-nots, speedwell, ground ivy and periwinkle; daisies, ladysmocks, stitchwort, deadnettle, wood sorrel and garlic mustard – the yellows, the blues and the whites – have all come at once. Hawthorn and blackthorn are out together; so, less publicly, are the pasque flower, the Loddon lily (summer snowflake) and the shy snakehead. The wild cherry vies with the larch, oak, maple, birch, poplar and alder to display its leaves and flowers simultaneously. Some appear fully-formed overnight in what is more like a stampede than the usual march of spring. Most typical of Berkshire perhaps are the breaking buds of beech that look like green moonbeams. It is all a bonus for the traveller with time to stand and stare. And a comfort to know that, like the lynchets on the hillsides – the last marks of the early commoner's plough – they may still be here when we have passed from the scene.

Beeches in Coombe Wood.

A Berkshire Bibliography

There is, of course, an alternative way of exploring the byways of Berkshire: that is through books. James Edmund Vincent's *Berkshire Byways* (1906) still ranks among the best. While you are reading Mr Vincent, you feel you are being introduced to all the best people in all the best places – and by the best possible guide. He has an Edwardian expansiveness, high-minded and lofty-toned without any of the air of a man pandering to popular taste. You can take it or leave it with him. He avails himself of the best modes of transport: the railway and the early motor car. He is a Wykehamist with an eye for the truly grand or picturesque that immediately exposes the trumpery or false. His mind dwells happily on Abingdon – puzzling over the paucity of its rail service, which has not improved since.

'To Abingdon, none the less, would I conduct the visitor by rail, having duly explained to him why he is entitled to say as much as he likes concerning the petty discomfort of the journey; and at Abingdon, for other reasons than that it is as tiresome to leave as to reach it, I would detain him sometime.'

Reading, though 'rich in railways and in history', is dismissed as 'a distressingly unlovely and bustling place, whereas at Windsor there is always the Castle to look at, and it never palls; and besides there is always the park, with its green turf and graceful deer, and stately, if not immemorial elms.' You feel he will head next for Stoke Poges and quote Thomas Gray, but he doesn't, disappointingly.

With P.H. Ditchfield, of yet earlier date, you can never be disappointed. He must have been one of those nineteenth century parsons who sat in their studies and wrote all the time. But then you realise that while he wrote or edited many books he travelled widely, too. He edited the *Victoria History of Berkshire* and sundry smaller books such as *Bygone Berkshire* as well as books on the villages and the manor houses of England – which are still in print. Part of *Bygone Berkshire* is devoted to bull-baiting at Wokingham – as gory an eyewitness account of a blood sport as Hemingway or clergyman – here the

Revd Canon Sturges – ever put his mind to. We are cushioned a little from the impending shock by a prelude stating that 'it was not until Christian teaching had been leavening society for 400 years that public opinion was educated up to the point of abolishing the gladiatorial contests, and the wholesale massacres of the Roman amphitheatre . . . Thus Shakespeare was silenced every Thursday, lest the bull-ring (in London) should be neglected.' But is this much protesting just a fanfare for the drama that is to come?

'The 21st of December, 1815, was a cold, damp, dull day. Two hours before noon, a young fellow drove out of Reading with a companion to see the Wokingham bull-baiting . . . Arrived at the Market Place, they joined the crowd of spectators filling every window, and in some cases seated on the roofs . . . A cry arises "room for the Alderman and Burgesses." The Alderman takes his seat and gives the signal that the sport is to begin . . . Here, he comes, the first bull, led by a dozen strong men, a rope round his horns and a chain fifteen feet long, into the middle of the market place, where the chain is fastened to a strong staple in a post level with the ground.'

The ensuing blood-and-thunder conflict between the dogs and the bull is amazingly vividly described. I have to remind myself that this canon of the Church of England is recalling something that happened, he says, only sixty years before the time of writing. Was he perhaps one of those youths who drove out of Reading on that cold, damp, dull, December day? We are spared not a drop of blood, not a crack of the thunderous hooves. 'It is now determined to dismiss the bull to the neighbouring slaughterhouse . . . The second bull is coming out fresh and strong, and good to keep up the sport for another hour or two. But we have seen enough, and may well return to Reading with our young friend . . .'

Alas, the clerical collar tightens and cramps his style at the end. 'Looking back on bull-baiting and similar sports,' he says, 'the conclusion cannot be escaped that the world's history shews a well-marked line at progress in the gentler virtues, and the growth of sympathy between man and his fellow, and between man and the animals around him, that tends to brand cruelty wherever found as a vice.' Fair – but, one finds oneself feeling, feeble enough.

Incidentally, while investigating Ditchfield in the *Dictionary of National Biography*, I came across the Revd David Davies, an earlier Rector of Barkham, near Reading, and – though I could not get hold of his book, *The Case of Labourers in Husbandry* – an even more remarkable man.

This Davies was born in Wales – as many of this name are – and he came from farming stock; but his career followed an extraordinary trajectory, taking him to college in Barbados as a charity scholar and, subsequently, usher and eventually headmaster. His upward flight seems, however, to have been checked by his reluctance to accept all the Church's doctrines and he became manager of a sugar plantation. Where better to witness the effects of hardship on the poor – and to resolve to do something about it? Instead of holy orders, he took a different sort of vow. He gave condemning evidence before a select committee on the African slave trade.

In about 1769 Davies returned to England as tutor to the nephew of a nabob, a friend of Robert Clive. He seems to have moved in influential circles, for, holy orders or not, in 1782 he was appointed Rector of Barkham, where he stayed for the rest of his life and wrote his well-received book.

Of all the books that sprouted from the earth at about this time – Arthur Young's *Travels*, Jethro Tull's *Horse-hoing Husbandry* and, of course Cobbett's *Rural Rides* (with scarcely a glance cast at Berkshire except to say how poor much of the land was) – Davies's *The Case of Labourers in Husbandry Stated and Considered* is the one I would most like to read. J.L. and Barbara Hammond praise it in *The Village Labourer 1760–1832*, a book that had an almost knock-out effect on me when I was young. I had scarcely heard of Newbury, let alone the Speenhamland System for poor relief propounded by a group of parsons and justices of the peace meeting in the Pelican Inn. Those ardent radicals, the Hammonds, condemned their kow-towing to the landowners, of course, but they acknowledged that the hands of

The Wind in the Willows.

this ad hoc body of well-meaning men were tied. Many of the farmers were tenants in awe of the larger landowners – the Cravens, the Carnarvons and the Ailesburys; and the landowners, powerful though they still were, had seen what happened to their brothers in France. As for the labourers, they were tied cottagers – tied hands, indeed!

As a footnote, it is interesting to observe that books on Berkshire have tended to occur about the beginning of each century. Along with Davies, Tull and Young came Mary Russell Mitford's *Our Village*; along with Hammond came *The Wind In The Willows* and *Three Men in a Boat*. At the beginning of this century, the millennium, came a host of commemorative publications, some of which portray desultory country pursuits but scarcely mention toil or soil. Exceptional, however, is the one with which I began this book: Aldermaston's *Memories* which is truly representative of the whole community and admirably reflects its earthy origins. Pure Berkshire, by the way!

Acknowledgements

In addition to the friendly people, named and unnamed, whom I met on my travels, I am most grateful to our excellent library and museum in Newbury where I have always found the staff unfailingly cheerful and obliging. I also owe much to The Friends of the Pang and Kennet Valleys, in particular to Dorcas Ward and Dick Greenaway, who do sterling work in propagating local knowledge besides reminding us of the needs as well as the delights of all such areas of outstanding natural beauty.

Finally, to Simon Fletcher, who commissioned this book, and to Michelle Tilling, who oversaw its publication, many thanks.